Lecture Notes in Economics and Mathematical Systems

411

Stéphane Dauzère-Péres   Jean-Bernard Lasserre

An Integrated Approach in Production Planning and Scheduling

Springer-Verlag

Berlin Heidelberg New York
London Paris Tokyo
Hong Kong Barcelona
Budapest

Authors

Dr. Stéphane Dauzère-Péres
Erasmus University Rotterdam
Rotterdam School of Management
Burg. Oudlaan 50 – P.O. Box 1738
3000 DR Rotterdam, The Netherlands

Jean-Bernard Lasserre
Directeur de Recherche
Centre National de la Recherche Scientifique (C.N.R.S.)
Laboratoire D'Automatique
et D'Analyse des Systèmes (L.A.A.S.)
7, av. du Colonel Roche
31077 Toulouse Cédex, France

658·5

D 24 L

ISBN 3-540-57905-2 Springer-Verlag Berlin Heidelberg New York
ISBN 0-387-57905-2 Springer-Verlag New York Berlin Heidelberg

CIP data applied for

© Springer-Verlag Berlin Heidelberg 1994
Printed in Germany

Typesetting: Camera ready by author
SPIN: 10090243   42/3140-543210 - Printed on acid-free paper

Acknowledgements

We express our gratitude to all our colleagues at the Laboratoire d'Automatique et d'Analyse des Systèmes (LAAS), who helped us refining the results presented in this book, including Prof. Jacky Erschler, Prof. Gérard Fontan, Dr. Jean-Claude Hennet, Dr. Pierre Lopez, Prof. Colette Mercé, Dr. François Roubellat, Dr. Gilbert de Terssac. We are also very grateful for the secretarial assistance provided by Eliane Dufour.

Furthermore, we thank Prof. Luk Van Wassenhove and Charles Corbett, from INSEAD, Prof. Marc Salomon from the Rotterdam School of Management, and Prof. Egon Balas from Carnegie-Mellon University, for their valuable comments.

Last but not least, we are very grateful for the continual support provided by our family.

Stéphane Dauzère-Péres is particularly indebted to Dr. Stanley B. Gershwin, who supported him during his stay at the Massachusetts Institute of Technology (MIT) in 1992-93, and with whom he always had fruitful discussions. He is also grateful to all the professors and colleagues he met at MIT or Boston University and particularly, Dr. N. Srivatsan, Dr. George Liberopoulos, Dr. Yves Dallery, Prof. Michael Caramanis, Prof. Ali Sharifnia, Mitchell Burman, Miltos Stamatopoulos. Finally, he would like to thank the French Foreign Office for its financial support through a Lavoisier fellowship.

The authors

Introduction

Production Management is a large field concerned with all the aspects related to production, from the very bottom decisions at the machine level, to the top-level strategic decisions. In this book, we are concerned with production planning and scheduling aspects.

Traditional production planning methodologies are based on a now widely accepted hierarchical decomposition into several planning decision levels. The higher in the hierarchy, the more aggregate are the models and the more important are the decisions. In this book, we only consider the last two decision levels in the hierarchy, namely, the mid-term (or *tactical*) planning level and the short-term (or *operational*) scheduling level. In the literature and in practice, the decisions are taken in sequence and in a **top-down** approach from the highest level in the hierarchy to the bottom level. The decisions taken at some level in the hierarchy are constrained by those already taken at upper levels and in turn, must translate into feasible objectives for the next lower levels in the hierarchy.

It is a common sense remark to say that the whole hierarchical decision process is *coherent* if the interactions between different levels in the hierarchy are taken into account so that a decision taken at some level in the hierarchy translates into a feasible objective for the next decision level in the hierarchy. However, and surprisingly enough, this crucial *consistency* issue is rarely investigated and few results are available in the literature.

Sometimes , the mid-term planning level itself is decomposed into two, aggregate and detailed, planning levels with models and decisions of the same nature. In this case, the consistency of decisions taken at those two levels has been investigated with success in the last twenty years. However, few results are available in the literature concerning consistency of planning and scheduling decisions. As quoted from a survey by J.K. Lenstra and A.H.G Rinnooy Kan *"There appear to be good opportunities for research on the interface between scheduling and inventory theory. Both ... have been developed in complete mutual isolation"*. As also noted by some authors, the need of a feasible master schedule is crucial for the success of an MRP (Material Requirement Planning) like procedure and *".. the lack of appropriate support for managers to produce good master schedules is a major weakness of MRP, and probably the biggest source of disappointment in the performance of such systems"*.

This consistency issue between planning and scheduling levels is the main motivation of the integrated planning and scheduling model presented in this book. In this integrated model, the plan computed at the planning level is **feasible**, *i.e.*, there exists at least one feasible schedule to achieve that production plan. To our knowledge, the approach as well as the results presented, are the first of this kind.

At the scheduling level, we propose a modified version of the *Shifting Bottleneck* procedure, known to be one the most efficient procedure so far for the general job-shop scheduling problem. Our modified version is based on an algorithm for the one-machine sequencing problem with general dependencies between jobs, not considered in the literature so far.

Finally, still at the scheduling level, we also present an integrated model for **lot streaming**, *i.e.*, when it is possible to split a lot into several sublots. An efficient and very simple solving procedure, similar in spirit to the one for computing a feasible plan, is described and tested on a sample.

This book is divided into six chapters. Basic models and methodologies in planning and scheduling are briefly outlined in Chapter I. In Chapter II, devoted to scheduling, the modified version (to be used in later chapters) of the Shifting Bottleneck procedure is presented. The integrated model for planning and scheduling is introduced in Chapter III along with a general solving procedure. Other solving procedures are presented in Chapter IV as well as experimental results. Some of these procedures should allow large-size models encountered in practice to be handled. In Chapter V, several model extensions are proposed and tested. Mainly, subcontracting (when backlogging is not allowed), and in-process inventories are considered. Finally, in Chapter VI, the integrated model for lot streaming in job-shop scheduling is introduced.

Table of Contents

Introduction   vii

Glossary   xiii

I   Production Planning and Scheduling   1

   I.1   Production Management 1
      I.1.1   The Production System 1
      I.1.2   The Management System 2
      I.1.3   Classification of Planning Decisions 3
   I.2   Production Planning 5
   I.3   Production Scheduling 8
   I.4   Planning and Scheduling 9
      I.4.1   Planning and Scheduling: Hierarchical Approaches 10
         I.4.1.1   Deterministic Approaches 10
         I.4.1.2   Stochastic Approaches 10
      I.4.2   Planning and Scheduling: Integrated Approaches 11
         I.4.2.1   The Economic Lot Scheduling Problem 11
         I.4.2.2   Simultaneous   Lotsizing   and   Scheduling [Afentakis 85] 12
         I.4.2.3   Interaction between Planning and Scheduling [Fontan and Imbert 85] 13
         I.4.2.4   Integrating Scheduling with Batching and Lotsizing [Potts and Van Wassenhove 92] 14
      I.4.3   Planning and Scheduling: Various Approaches 15
   I.5   Conclusion 16

II   Job-Shop Sequencing and Scheduling   17

   II.1   Introduction 17
   II.2   Job-Shop Scheduling 18
      II.2.1   Definitions 18
      II.2.2   Exact Methods 21
      II.2.3   Heuristic Procedures 23
         II.2.3.1   List Scheduling Algorithms 23

      II.2.3.2 Other Methods 23
II.3 The Shifting Bottleneck Procedure 24
    II.3.1 Introduction 24
    II.3.2 The Shifting Bottleneck Procedure 25
    II.3.3 The One-Machine Sequencing Problem 27
        II.3.3.1 Introduction 27
        II.3.3.2 Carlier's Algorithm 27
    II.3.4 Remarks on the Shifting Bottleneck Procedure 29
II.4 A Modified Shifting Bottleneck Procedure 30
    II.4.1 Drawbacks of the Shifting Bottleneck Procedure 30
    II.4.2 The Dependent Job Algorithm 33
    II.4.3 A Modified Shifting Bottleneck Procedure 39
    II.4.4 Computational Experiments 40
        II.4.4.1 The 10×10 and 5×20 Classical Examples 40
        II.4.4.2 Computational Results 40
    II.4.5 Conclusion 42
II.5 A Priority Rule-Based Dispatching Heuristic 42
II.6 Conclusion 43

III An Integrated Planning and Scheduling Model   **45**
III.1 Introduction 45
III.2 Notation and Definitions 47
    III.2.1 Job-Shop Scheduling 47
    III.2.2 Planning 49
III.3 Integrating Planning and Scheduling Decisions 51
    III.3.1 Introduction 51
    III.3.2 Multi-Period Scheduling 52
    III.3.3 A Linear Model in Continuous Variables 55
    III.3.4 Necessary Conditions 56
    III.3.5 Sufficient Conditions 57
    III.3.6 An Integrated Model with Set-Up Times 58
III.4 Solving Procedures 59
    III.4.1 A One-Pass Procedure 59
    III.4.2 An Iterative Procedure 60
        III.4.2.1 Introduction 60
        III.4.2.2 The Procedure 61
        III.4.2.3 The Scheduling Problem 62
        III.4.2.4 Convergence Properties 63
III.5 First Computational Results 65
    III.5.1 With no Set-Up Time 65
    III.5.2 With Set-Up Times 67
    III.5.3 Other Computational Results 67
III.6 Conclusion 70

IV Various Resolution Strategies   **71**

IV.1 Introduction 71

IV.2 Two Multi-Period Scheduling Policies 71

    IV.2.1 The Global Scheduling Policy 72

        IV.2.1.1 The Modified Shifting Bottleneck (MSB) Procedure . 74

        IV.2.1.2 A Priority Rule-Based Dispatching (PRD) Heuristic 79

        IV.2.1.3 Comparison between the Two Scheduling Methods . 81

    IV.2.2 The Period by Period Scheduling Policy 81

        IV.2.2.1 The Modified Shifting Bottleneck (MSB) Procedure . 84

        IV.2.2.2 A Priority Rule-Based Dispatching (PRD) Heuristic 87

        IV.2.2.3 Comparison between the Two Scheduling Methods . 87

    IV.2.3 Comparison between the Two Scheduling Policies 90

    IV.2.4 Other Multi-Period Scheduling Policies 92

IV.3 Influence of the Backlogging Cost 93

IV.4 Rolling Horizon 94

V Extensions of the Model   **97**

V.1 Introduction 97

V.2 Subcontracting 97

    V.2.1 Model Modifications 98

    V.2.2 Experimental Results 99

V.3 Work-In-Process Inventories 99

    V.3.1 Model Modifications 99

    V.3.2 Experimental Results 104

V.4 Lot Streaming Option 105

    V.4.1 Model Modifications 106

V.5 Conclusion 106

VI Lot Streaming   **107**

VI.1 Introduction 107

VI.2 A Lot-Streaming Procedure 109

    VI.2.1 Notation and Definitions 109

    VI.2.2 An Integrated Model 110

    VI.2.3 An Iterative Procedure 111

    VI.2.4 The Rounding Procedure 113

    VI.2.5 The Model with Set-Up Times 113

    VI.2.6 A Lower Bound 114

VI.3 Computational Results 114

    VI.3.1 The 6×6 and 10×10 Problems 115

    VI.3.2 Test on a Sample 116

    VI.3.3 With Set-Up Times 120

    VI.3.4 CPU Time and Number of Iterations 121

VI.4 Impact on Lotsizing Models 125

VI.5 Conclusion 125

Conclusion   **127**

Bibliography   **129**

List of Figures   **135**

List of Tables   **137**

Glossary

The notation used in this book are briefly defined below. Reference to the chapter where they are used for the first time is indicated.

CHAPTER I

m : number of machines (resources).

$M = \{1, .., m\}$: the set of the machines.

n : nomber of products.

J_i : job (lot) associated to product i.

$J = \{J_1, .., J_n\}$: the set of jobs.

r_i : realease date of job J_i.

d_i : due date of job J_i.

o_{ijk} : j^{th} operation of job J_i to be processed on machine k.

t_{ijk} : start time of operation o_{ijk}.

p_{ijk} : processing time of operation o_{ijk}.

C_i : completion date of job J_i.

$L_i = C_i - d_i$: lateness (algebraic delay) of job J_i.

$T_i = max(0, L_i)$: tardiness (real delay) of job J_i.

C_{max} : makespan.

X_i^u : lot-size for product i for a basic period.

X_i^t : total amount of product i to be delivered by the end of period t.

n_i : number of lots of size X_i^u needed to produce X_i^t.

CHAPTER II

$G = (N, A, E)$: disjunctive graph.

N : set of nodes of G.

A : set of conjunctive arcs of G.

E_k : set of disjunctive arcs of G associated with machine k.

$E = \bigcup_{k \in M} E_k$: set of disjunctive arcs of G.

S_k : selection in E_k.

$S = \bigcup\limits_{k \in M} S_k$: complete selection in E.

$G_S = (N, A, S)$: conjunctive graph associated with selection S.

M_0 : set of machines already sequenced.

$O(k, M_0)$: scheduling problem associated with machine k.

$v(k, M_0)$: criterion of problem $O(k, M_0)$.

$l(o_{ijk}, o_{i'j'k'})$: length of the longest path between operations o_{ijk} and $o_{i'j'k'}$.

r_{ijk} : release date of operation o_{ijk}.

q_{ijk} : remaining time in the workshop after operation o_{ijk}.

J^* : set of jobs to be processed on a machine.

U : set of jobs already scheduled.

$\overline{U}$: set of remaining jobs to be scheduled ($J^* = U \cup \overline{U}$).

J_c : critical job.

I : critical set.

v : node in a tree.

V : set of nodes in a tree.

f_v : lower bound associated with node v.

f^{sup} : upper bound.

y : sequence of jobs on the machines.

IC : critical path.

$\{S_{so}\}$: set of operations that may be scheduled.

$\{S_{so}^k\}$: set of operations that may be scheduled on machine k.

$\{S_{ip}\}$: set of "in-progress" operations.

$\{S_{ip}^k\}$: set of "in-progress" operations on machine k.

CHAPTER III

From chapter III, some notation is changed to incorporate the notion of period.

H : planning horizon.

T : number of periods in the planning horizon.

c_t : number of time units available in period t.

D_{it} : demand of product i, at period t.

X_{it} : amount of product i to be delivered by the end of period t.

I_{it} : inventory level of product i, at the end of period t.

$g(X, I)$: criterion to minimize.

I_{it}^+ : real on-hand inventory of product i at the end of period t.

I_{it}^- : backlog of product i at the end of period t.

c_{it}^+ : per unit holding cost.

c_{it}^- : per unit backlog cost.

c_{it}^{pr} : per unit production cost.

I_0 : initial inventory.

$P = (X_{11}, X_{12}, .., X_{nT})$: production plan.

Y : set of admissible sequences.

J_{it} : job associated with product i, to be completed by the end of period t.

$J^t = \{J_{1t}, .., J_{nt}\}$: set of jobs to be completed by the end of period t.

$J = \{J^1, .., J^T\}$: set of jobs.

o_{ijkt} : operation of a job at period t.

p_{ijkt}^u : per unit processing time of operation o_{ijkt}.

p_{ijkt}^t : processing time of operation o_{ijkt}.

τ_{ijkt} : set-up time of operation o_{ijkt}.

t_{ijkt} : starting time of operation o_{ijkt}.

L : set of last operations in the routing.

O_{kt} : set of operations of period t to be processed on machine k.

Ω : set of admissible plans.

$S(y)$: complete selection associated with sequence y.

s_{it} : boolean variable $:= 1$ if $X_{it} > 0$ and 0 otherwise.

Δ_{it} : set-up cost of job J_{it}.

$R(y_k, P^k)$: set of active capacity constraints.

l_{it} : length of a fictitious arc issuing from the last operation i the routing of job J_{it}.

CHAPTER V

T_{it} : tardiness of job J_i at period t.

X_{it}^+ : amount of product i to be processed by the end of period t in the workshop.

X_{it}^- : amount of product i subcontracted at period t.

c_{it}^{st} : per unit subcontracting cost.

N_{it} : set of operations in the routing of job J_i at period t.

A_{it} : set of pairs of operations of job J_i at period t constrained by precedence relations.

Q_{ijkt} : WIP inventory between operation o_{ijkt} and the next operation in the routing of job J_{it}.

Q_{it} : sum of all teh WIP inventories in period t.

F : set of firts operations in the routing.

c_{ijkt}^{int} : per unit holding cost in WIP inventory Q_{ijkt}.

c_{it}^{int} : per unit holding cost in WIP inventory Q_{it}.

Chapter I

Production Planning and Scheduling

I.1   Production Management

Production Management is concerned with all the various aspects related to an efficient organization of the production process of goods or services. In this work, we only consider the production planning issues in manufacturing processes. The interested reader is referred to *e.g.*, [Hax and Candea 84], [Giard 88], [Conway *et al.* 67], for a more detailed treatment of the various planning and scheduling models. Here, we only briefly outline the planning and scheduling decision levels, along with various standard approaches to handle both levels.

It is very common to separate the management system from the production system. In the former, one deals with *flows* of information whereas, in the latter, one deals with *flows* of products (see Figure I-1).

I.1.1   The Production System

The production system contains all the resources (workers as well as machines) required to transform some raw material into finished products. Included in the production system are the storage facilities and sometimes the distribution facilities.

Production systems may be characterized according to two typologies [Giard 88], although they are not the only ones.

In the first typology, one distinguishes between **make-to-order** and **make-to-stock** production systems. In the former, the production is based on customer orders whereas, in the latter, the production is based on an anticipation of the customer orders.

Make-to-order production systems are primarily found in companies that propose a large variety of products for which the demand is not predictable over a long horizon, or in companies that define their products only from precise customer requirements. Subcontracting companies are a typical example of the latter.

Make-to-stock production is only possible in companies where the catalogue of products is relatively stable in time, and more importantly, where the demand for such products is relatively well identified. Moreover, in general, the production cycle is larger than the time interval between the customer order and the desired delivery date. And the eventual jumps in the demand do not necessitate an increase in the production capacity if they are taken into account soon enough. The automobile industry is a good example of such production systems.

The second typology distinguishes between four different types of production (see [Bénassy 87]):

1. **Unitary Production:** The large size of the finished product imposes a production of small quantities, and the main task is to provide all the production resources when and where necessary. In this type of production (for example, rockets, aircraft, submarines ...), one uses *Project Management* techniques.

2. **Production in small and medium series:** The finished product has a smaller size, and the manufacturing process usually takes place in a workshop. The problem is not to minimize the total time for producing one item but rather the whole production, and a related goal is to minimize the waiting time in front of the resources.

3. **Production in large series:** In the case where there is a large number of similar products to be produced in the same period of time, or when the number of different products is limited, it may be interesting to organize *transfer lines* of production where the resources are distributed according to a fixed ordering. In doing so, one can reduce the waiting time in front of the resources. The main problem is thus to create equilibrate transfer lines (**line balancing**)

4. **Continuous Production:** In this case, the transfer line is *continuous, i.e.,* any waiting time between the resources is excluded. This type of production occurs for example when one has to manipulate liquids or gas. Again, a good *line balancing* is necessary for efficiency.

In all the following chapters, we are mainly interested in *make-to-stock* production in small and medium series, or in *make-to-order* production where the demand is well-defined over a certain horizon.

I.1.2   The Management System

Usually, the interactions between the management system, the production system and their environment may be represented as in Figure I-1.

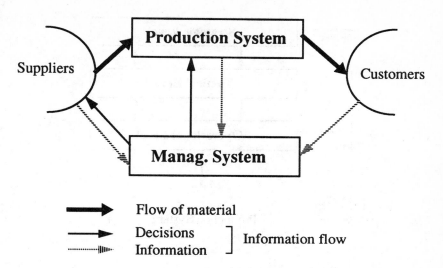

Figure I-1: Interactions between management system, production system and environment.

On one side, the suppliers provide the production system with raw material according to the decisions from the management system. Then, the intermediate products circulate in the production system on the resources, and may wait in Work-In-Process inventories (buffers). Finally, the finished products wait in stocks before delivery to the customers. Sometimes, the management system also controls the transport of material before and after the production process.

The management system negotiates customer orders and according to them, determines the production plan while taking supplier constraints into account. Moreover, one of its essential features is to control the production system by taking possible perturbations into account by feedback.

The various decisions taken in the management system are very different in nature, and are related to different decision levels. Below, one finds a classification of the planning decisions, now largely accepted in the production management community.

I.1.3   Classification of Planning Decisions

Usually, the planning decisions belong to three main decision levels (Figure I-2), with proper time horizons: Strategic level, tactical level, and operational level (see [Anthony 65] or [Bitran and Tirupati 93]).

- *Strategic level*
  It deals with the general policy of the company. The decisions at this level

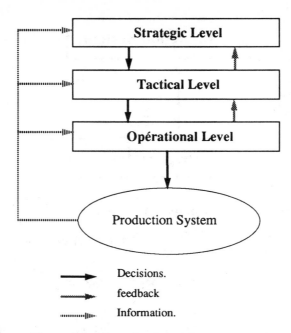

Figure I-2: Three-level decision structure.

involve top-level managers and concern the size and location of new plants, new resource acquisition, the choice of new products .... The information is highly aggregated, and its source is largely external. The strategic decisions, often taken for several years, are constraints for the lower decision levels.

- *Tactical level*
  Resources are allocated to manufacture various products in order to satisfy customer orders. The time horizon is usually expressed in months or weeks. The information is moderately aggregated, and its source is external and internal. Again, the tactical decisions become constraints for the operational level.

Usually, a production plan is determined over a 3 to 18 months time horizon. Sometimes, an *aggregation* of products into families (when the number of products is very large) is useful (see [Bitran and Tirupati 93] or [Merce 87]). In this production plan, the quantities to produce at each period of the horizon (a period usually varies from a week to a month) are calculated so that one tries to satisfy the demand while minimizing production and holding costs (and perhaps some other criteria). The planning decisions are of the type *how much* to produce at each period.

- *Operational level*

  The decisions at this level deal with the organization of the work on the production resources in the workshop, to achieve the goal specified by the tactical level. The time horizon is shorter (from several days to several weeks). The information is detailed, and its source is largely internal. First, a disaggregation of the aggregate plan is necessary if the goal is given in terms of aggregate products. The scheduling of products on the machines, and the routing of the vehicles are typical decisions.

  At this level, we are interested in the scheduling problem, *i.e.*, in finding a schedule of the operations on the products so that all the conflicts on the resources are resolved. The scheduling decisions are of the type *how and when* to produce.

This hierarchical model is not always exact since in some cases, certain decisions can be taken more or less early in the hierarchy. Broadly speaking, the higher the level of the decisions, the more important the impact of these decisions on the revenue of the company.

Most of the time, the decisions at each level are taken in *sequence*, *i.e.*, in a **top-down** approach, and, for example, nothing guarantees that the production plan computed at the tactical level is an achievable objective for the operational level. This partly explains large Work-In-Process inventories and delivery delays for customers in today's factories. Indeed, no matter how sophisticated is the scheduling method used at the operational level, it will be of a limited efficiency if the objective given by the tactical level is not realistic.

This consistency issue between the planning and scheduling decision levels is the main motivation of the integrated model for job-shop planning and scheduling to be presented in later chapters. We label this model *integrated* because we integrate in the planning model constraints that ensure that the production plan is **feasible**. By feasible, we mean that there exists at least one feasible schedule compatible with that plan, *i.e.*, a schedule such that the jobs corresponding to the production plan are completed by their due date.

Before presenting this integrated planning and scheduling model, we first briefly outline the main different planning and scheduling methodologies. Then, the main hierarchical approaches with their drawbacks are briefly reviewed, and finally some of the few integrated models are also presented.

I.2   Production Planning

Before planning the production, some information relative to the production system is needed, in particular the set of demands over the planning horizon. If the demands are not known exactly, a preliminary forecast study is necessary and, of course, the quality of the planning decisions will depend on the quality of the forecast.

Then, a production plan can be computed in taking account of the constraints imposed by the strategic level.

When the size of the planning problem is too large, it is often necessary to use some **aggregation** concepts (see [Bitran and Tirupati 93] for a survey). A set of variables sharing some common characteristic is replaced by a single *aggregate* variable. There are various types of aggregations (on the resources, on the products, ...). However, the aggregate plan must be *feasible*, *i.e.*, there must exist at least one *coherent* disaggregation yielding a feasible detailed production plan. Again, this is a coherence issue between two planning decision levels and it has been investigated by several authors (see [Bitran and Tirupati 93], [Merce 87]).

A typical MPS model is as follows (see [Hax and Candea 84]):

$$
\begin{cases}
min\sum_{t=1}^{T}\sum_{i=1}^{n}(c_{it}^{+}.I_{it}^{+} + c_{it}^{-}.I_{it}^{-} + c_{it}^{pr}.X_{it}) + \sum_{t=1}^{T}(r_t.R_t + o_t.O_t) \\
(I_{it}^{+} - I_{it}^{-}) - (I_{it-1}^{+} - I_{it-1}^{-}) - X_{it} + D_{it} & = 0 & i = 1,..,n; t = 1,..,T & (1) \\
X_{it} & \geq 0 & \forall i, t & (2) \\
I_{it}^{+} & \geq 0 & \forall i, t & (3) \\
I_{it}^{-} & \geq 0 & \forall i, t & (4) \\
\sum_{i=1}^{n}(m_i.X_{it}) & \leq R_t + O_t & t = 1,..,T & (5) \\
R_t & \leq rm_t & t = 1,..,T & (6) \\
O_t & \leq om_t & t = 1,..,T & (7) \\
R_t & \geq 0 & \forall t & (8) \\
O_t & \geq 0 & \forall t & (9)
\end{cases}
$$

where

T is the number of periods in the planning horizon.

n is the number of products.

X_{it} is the production of product i in period t.

D_{it} is the demand for product i at period t.

$I_{it} = I_{it}^{+} - I_{it}^{-}$ is the inventory of product i at the end of period t.

I_{it}^{+} is the physical inventory of product i on hand at the end of period t.

I_{it}^{-} is the shortage (or backlog) of product i at the end of period t.

c_{it}^{+} (respectively c_{it}^{-}) is the per unit holding (respectively backlogging) cost for product i at period t.

c_{it}^{pr} is the per unit production cost for product i in period t.

R_t (respectively O_t) is the number of *regular* (respectively *overtime*) hours used in period t.

r_t (respectively o_t) is the per unit cost of a *regular* (respectively *overtime*) production hour in period t.

m_i is the number of hours needed to process one unit of product i.

rm_t (respectively om_t) is the maximum number of available *regular* (respectively *overtime*) hours in period t.

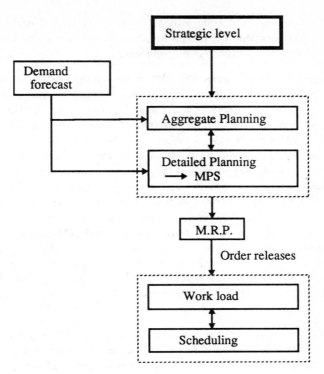

Figure I-3: Typical production planning approach.

The reader is also referred to [Salomon 91] for various lotsizing models.

In a typical production planning approach, the detailed production plan MPS (or **Master Production Schedule**) is computed, and then an MRP interface (**Material Requirement Planning**) is used to determine release dates of the jobs in the workshop and the timing and quantities of raw material that are required (see [Orlicky 75]).

MRP. In a MRP module, the production plan (MPS) is *propagated backwards* through the routing (from end-products to raw material), while taking the *lead-times* between stages as well as initial inventories into account. In the propagation, some more or less sophisticated *lotsizing* policy may be used in the computation of the lot-sizes of various components. For instance, assume that an end-product is made of two components with a one week lead-time, and also assume that 100 (resp. 50) units of this end-product must be delivered the first week (resp. second week). In a lot-for-lot lotsizing policy, 100 units of both components must be available at the end of the previous week, and 50 others at the end of the first week. In this simple case, with this lot-for-lot policy and a zero initial inventory, the production plan for each component is the end-product one, *shifted* one week to the right (*i.e.*, anticipated) to take the lead time into account. Similarly, if each component is itself made of other components, the production objective just calculated is in turn propagated backwards until there is no predecessor.

As quoted in [Hax and Candea 84], *"MRP accepts the master schedule as an input, assumes that it is feasible from the view-point of the resource requirements, and plans orders of component items accordingly."* Therefore, among the requirements that have to be met to give a MRP implementation project a chance of success *" .. A feasible master production schedule must be drawn up, or else the accumulated planned orders of components might "bump" into the resource restrictions and become infeasible. [Smith 78] points out that the lack of appropriate support for managers to produce good master schedules is a major weakness of MRP, and probably the biggest source of disappointment in the performance of such systems."*
In the case where the MPS violates some resource capacities, adjustment of the MPS is then possible in certain **MRP II or CRP (Capacity Requirement Planning)** systems. However, to detect these capacity violations, those systems take into account only rough capacity constraints, *i.e.*, they mainly check if the total amount of work required on each machine is less than the capacity. In particular, the sequencing of jobs on the machines, a crucial information for detailed capacity, is ignored.

According to the length of the planning horizon, the MPS is calculated at the tactical level or at the operational level. If computed at the tactical level, a finer determination of lot-sizes may be necessary at the operational level.

Finally, at the operational level, one must organize the work on the machines so that the production quantities determined in the MPS are effectively produced in time. This is a scheduling problem.

I.3   Production Scheduling

At the operational level, the **lots** of items determined in the MPS must be effectively produced. Those lots, called **jobs** in the workshop, have to be processed on various resources at different stages of the manufacturing process, before becoming lots of *finished products*. The processing of a job on a specific resource is called an *operation* (or task). A *schedule* consists of a pair of start time and completion time for each operation, *i.e.*, the time interval during which the job is on the resource. A schedule is called *feasible* if no two time intervals associated to the same resource or the same job overlap. Often, to be feasible, a schedule also needs to meet some additional requirements on the jobs and the production process, according to the problem considered, *e.g.* release dates, number of machines, storage areas between machines (buffers), ... Solving a scheduling problem is determining a feasible schedule that optimizes a given criterion. Such a schedule is called *optimal*. Scheduling problems can be designated using the three-field classification $\alpha|\beta|\gamma$ presented in [Lawler *et al.* 93]. The first field α describes the machine environment, the second field β presents the job characteristics, and the last field γ specifies the optimality criterion. For a complete treatment of the subject, the reader is referred to [Lawler *et al.* 93].

Three main types of workshops are considered in the literature on scheduling. In a *Flow-Shop*, all the products visit the machines with the same ordering. In a *Job-Shop*, for each job, the order in which the operations are processed (*routing*) is fixed, but not necessarily the same. In an *Open-Shop*, less frequently studied in the literature, each job must still be processed on a fixed set of machines, but the routing is not fixed.

In the next chapter, we consider the job-shop scheduling problem $J||C_{max}$ (see Section II.2.1), where C_{max}, called the *makespan*, denotes the completion time of all jobs. **Exact** algorithms (see Section II.2.2) for solving this problem are usually based on *Branch and Bound* techniques. However, these methods require significant computing times, and they are not able to solve realistic size problems.

For this reason, **heuristic** procedures (see Section II.2.3) are developed. Roughly speaking, they belong to three main classes:

1. *List scheduling* algorithms. They are the simplest to implement. Operations are assigned to machines according to some priority rules.

2. In the second class, one finds methods that solve the multi-machine problem by iteratively solving one-machine scheduling problems. The *Shifting Bottleneck Procedure* of [Adams *et al.* 88] is the most representative method in this class. This procedure has been recognized as one of the most efficient heuristic so far, and is described in detail in Section II.3. We propose an improved version in Section II.4

3. The other methods fall into the class of **local search** algorithms. *Simulated Annealing* and *Taboo Search* are among the most popular methods in this class. General purpose methods, they are very simple to implement, but require often a huge amount of computation in order to yield good results.

I.4 Planning and Scheduling

Many manufacturing companies do not have a systematic production planning procedure. Often, the customer order is directly translated into a single lot of items to be processed. There is neither possible splitting (lotsizing) of this lot nor possible grouping (batching) of several small orders (sometimes there may be some managerial reasons to do so). If any lotsizing or batching procedure is to be applied, it uses some *rule-of-the-thumb* technique. The lots are then released in the workshop according to some scheduling procedure. Of course, nothing guarantees that the lots of finished products will be delivered on time.

A hierarchical decomposition of the planning and scheduling procedure simplifies the problem. However, most of the planning models in such a decomposition have a very aggregate view of the workshop and ignore crucial constraints induced by the scheduling level. Therefore, *consistency* of the whole decision process is not ensured. As already mentioned, nothing guarantees that the planning procedure at the tactical level provides the scheduling level with a feasible objective. An integrated approach is certainly more complex but eliminates this drawback.

I.4.1 Planning and Scheduling: Hierarchical Approaches

I.4.1.1 Deterministic Approaches

In a typical approach, one first determines a *Master Production Schedule* (MPS) based on the forecasted demands, and with some resource constraints. A **CRP** or **MRP II** interface sometimes refines the MPS by taking some more detailed capacity constraints into account. However, for example, the sequencing issue is totally ignored whereas it has a crucial impact on the real effective capacity of the workshop. In other words, *how much* (a tactical decision) can be produced strongly depends on *how and when* these quantities are produced. Even if the lot-sizes are refined, the existence of a feasible schedule is not guaranteed. As noted in [Buxey 89], *"the planning, MRP and scheduling modules are used in sequence and are poorly integrated"*.

Later in this book, we present an integrated model in which the planning level model takes account of detailed capacity constraints, in such a manner that existence of a feasible schedule is guaranteed. Such a feasible schedule is only proposed to the scheduling level which may still chooses another one.

I.4.1.2 Stochastic Approaches

Using a time-scale decomposition, well-known in Control Theory, [Gershwin 89] has developed a hierarchical continuous time model where the inputs and outputs of each module in the hierarchy consist of **rates** (production rates, maintenance rates, failure rates, set-up rates, ...). The output of a module is a **policy**, *e.g.*, production rates $u(x)$ which depend on x, the state of the system. Indeed, due to random events such as failures, the state of the system is unpredictable, and the decisions (as for instance, production rates u) have to depend on the state x.

The different levels in the hierarchy correspond to classes of *events* and *decisions* with different frequencies. For example, in many cases, the maintenance decisions are far less frequent than some types of failures (uncontrollable events), which in turn are far less frequent than the decisions of assigning an item to a machine (controllable event) etc .... The higher in the hierarchy, the less frequent the events treated at this level. Also, in a given level, the variables that vary slowly (*i.e.*, proper to some upper level) are considered constant at their value at the time considered. The effect of variables that vary faster (*i.e.*, proper to some lower level) is "averaged out".

In a production context, this kind of hierarchical model is well suited to situations of large *continuous productions*, *i.e.*, when the transfer batch consists of few items (ideally one). In this case, when an item in a lot has been processed on some machine it does not wait for the other items of the lot before going to the downstream machine so that the sequencing issue is not crucial. When the production is by (possibly large) lots, this model may not be appropriate.

I.4.2 Planning and Scheduling: Integrated Approaches

Some methods have already tried to treat simultaneously planning and scheduling issues. Their main drawback is the (small) size of the problems that can be solved.

An old standard management problem in the literature on production is the famous one-machine ELSP (Economic Lot Scheduling Problem) in continuous time. Despite numerous efforts, characterizing an optimal solution to this, at first glance simple, problem is still an open issue. It is in part responsible for the splitting of the research community into a Lotsizing and a Scheduling community.

More recently, [Afentakis 85] has proposed a model that, in principle, would determine simultaneously lot-sizes and a schedule for a job-shop.

Using a two-level hierarchical model, [Fontan and Imbert 85] have developed an approach that can be qualified *integrated* since the output is a production plan over some discretized horizon along with a feasible schedule for the first period of the horizon.

Finally, [Potts and Van Wassenhove 92] have presented a model in which batching and lotsizing decisions as well as sequencing decisions could be calculated simultaneously. However, no methodology is proposed.

I.4.2.1 The Economic Lot Scheduling Problem

The ELSP problem has the following characteristics ([Zipkin 91]):

- Several products must be processed on a single machine which can process only one product at a time.

- There is a constant demand rate, and demand must be filled immediately. Production also occurs at a constant rate and there may be a set-up time before production can start.

- For each product, the holding cost rate is constant and there may also be a set-up cost.

- A schedule to be determined must include a complete specification of which products are to be processed, as well as how much and when. The criterion is the long-run average cost.

This problem has attracted a lot of attention in the literature, and despite its apparent simplicity, is in fact very difficult to solve. There are mainly two kinds of approaches which either

- determine an optimal solution to a simplified problem, or

- determine *good* solutions to the original problem.

Most of the proposed solutions restrict to certain classes of policies, mainly the class of *cyclic* schedules where the schedule is designed so that the entire system is periodic. One may distinguish two main variants (see [Zipkin 91] or [Elmaghraby 78]):

1. One chooses a **basic period,** and states that the cycle time of each product is an integer multiple of this basic period. Moreover, all the products can be processed in a basic period.

2. One determines a **common cycle time** (for all the products), sufficiently large to ensure that at least the production of one item of each product can occur in a cycle. Sometimes, one may impose that a product can be processed only once in a cycle.

In all the cases, it is a single machine problem which restricts its potential applications. As a matter of fact, the relative lack of strong results for this apparently simple problem, partly explains why, most of the time, lotsizing and scheduling are treated independently.

I.4.2.2　Simultaneous　　　Lotsizing　　and　　Scheduling [Afentakis 85]

For a job-shop, [Afentakis 85] translates a production planning problem into a scheduling problem. He uses the notion of **basic period** in which, if a resource processes some product, then it processes only that product. The graph of the routing of a product is a tree (assembly is permitted), in which a node corresponds to the manufacturing of a product on a machine. The final products (without successors in the graph) must satisfy a certain known demand.

The lot-size (X_i^u) for product i is equal to the maximum number of items that can be processed in a *basic period*. Manufacturing X_i^t means manufacturing n_i lots of product i $(X_i^t \le n_i.X_i^u)$. The integer number n_i is computed so that the corresponding demand is satisfied. The basic period being the constant common processing time of all the lots, they are treated as operations of unitary duration. The initial problem is thus translated into a job-shop scheduling problem with due date constraints, and sequencing constraints between lots of the same product and between lots of adjacent products in the graph. Moreover, there is a holding cost per basic period where an operation is completed before its due date. The goal is to minimize the weighted lateness (actually earliness) criterion. Thus, in an optimal schedule, the demands are filled, the capacity constraints are satisfied, and the holding cost is minimized. If there exists no feasible schedule, the problem is not solvable (at least for the chosen basic period).

However, it should be noticed that the *basic period* is chosen independently of the schedule. Once again, in this model, the choice of the basic period, *i.e.*, the lot-sizes, is crucial and does not ensure the existence of a feasible schedule. Finally, it must be noted that the size of the problem may rapidly become a major drawback.

I.4.2.3   Interaction between Planning and Scheduling [Fontan and Imbert 85]

In a two-level hierarchical model, the upper MPS type (planning) level determines a production plan over a finite horizon discretized into periods, and the lower (scheduling) level determines whether there exists a feasible schedule only in the first period of the horizon. Simulation, using some given priority rules, is used at the lower level.

If there is no feasible schedule in the first period, this information is fed back to the upper level and some capacity parameters are modified. For example, the number of working hours at some machine is increased, or the planned quantity to process in the first period is decreased.

One iterates this procedure (Figure I-4) until convergence to a feasible plan occurs.

This approach assumes that it is always possible to increase the number of working hours. Also, the number of iterations may rapidly become very large for highly constrained problems.

The approach that we propose later is close in spirit to this approach.

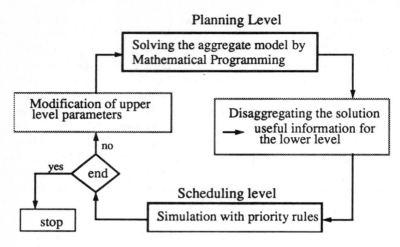

Figure I-4: Iterative procedure.

I.4.2.4   Integrating   Scheduling   with   Batching   and Lotsizing [Potts and Van Wassenhove 92]

Here, we consider a standard scheduling problem. In [Potts and Van Wassenhove 92], **batching** means grouping together several lots with same processing characteristics on a machine so that some set-up time can be saved. On the other hand, **lotsizing** means possible splitting of large lots into smaller lots.

They also observe that there is no links between *scheduling* on the one side, and *batching* and *lotsizing* on the other side. As quoted from [Potts and Van Wassenhove 92], *".. both worlds seem to be very much apart. The scheduling literature nearly always assume that batching and lotsizing decisions are already taken. Similarly, research on batching and lotsizing seldom considers sequencing issues."*

In the model described in [Potts and Van Wassenhove 92], the batching and lotsizing decisions, as well as the sequencing decisions, must be taken *simultaneously*. The model is presented for *flow-shops* and *open-shops*. The goal is to improve the scheduling of a fixed plan by using lotsizing and batching techniques. They conclude that no existing methodology so far, is likely to help in solving such a difficult problem.

The paper concludes with a survey of the few existing methods for integrated scheduling and batching on the one side, and integrated scheduling and lotsizing on the other side. Most of the work is concerned with one machine, at most two machines for flow-shops or open-shops, or identical parallel machines.

I.4.3 Planning and Scheduling: Various Approaches

Many production management models have been developed. It is not the scope of this book to review all the existing models and methods. However, in this section, we briefly mention some of them (see [Aggarwal 91]).

In the early eighties, a software package named **OPT** (Optimized Production Technology) came out with some success. Roughly speaking, the OPT philosophy is to identify the bottleneck machines and concentrate on them, *i.e.*, optimize their utilization. However, the production plan must be feasible anyway. OPT has been tried in many american companies. However, it has to face some critics as it works as a *black box*. Moreover, many users contest what the designers claim and have had a limited success so far ([Aggarwal 91]).

The **JIT** (Just-In-Time) concept has been developed in Japan since 1945 and in the USA and Europe since 1980. *Kanban*, the most representative method, has been introduced by Toyota in the automobile industry. JIT methods are primarily intended for *repetitive* productions in which the cycle time of the products is relatively small. The goal is to produce only what is required (the demand is perfectly identified) and at the last possible moment. Rather than a precise technical procedure, JIT is more a philosophy where everybody in the workshop has to participate. It demands a radical change in the attitudes, and requires a strong cooperation between salesmen, executives and employees (see for instance [Golhar and Stamm 91]).

A simple kanban system is illustrated in Figure I-5. The flow of products circulates through workstations from the left (raw material) to the right (end-product) whereas the flow of kanbans circulates the other way. To each item entering a workstation is attached a kanban, which is taken off and put in the kanban buffer of the upstream machine when the item is leaving the workstation. Therefore, each workstation has two output buffers. One is fed in products by the workstation when a product has been processed, and the other is fed in kanbans by the downstream workstation when a product is leaving that workstation.

Again, so far, few american companies have implemented JIT with a real success ([Aggarwal 91]). Moreover, the difficult problem is sent back to an upper level in charge of the conception of the workshop (determination of the number of kanbans for example).

Finally, **CIM** is a new concept that emerged in the mid eighties. **Integration** is the main focus, and virtually concerns all the issues treated separately in previous approaches. Some expert systems have been developed to evaluate different alternatives relating various issues such as assembly, sales, purchases,...

Too few practical results exist that would permit to conclude if this ambitious approach is viable.

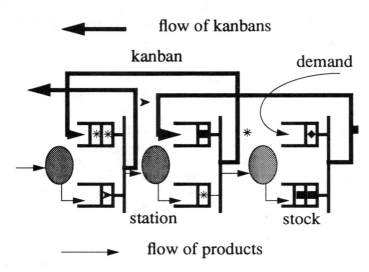

Figure I-5: A simple kanban system

I.5   Conclusion

For a long time, research in production planning has mainly considered hierarchical planning approaches for it seemed too difficult (and perhaps not desirable) to integrate in a unique model various decisions, different in nature. On the one hand, this approach is appealing since it decomposes the whole problem into simpler problems to solve. On the other hand, by treating each decision level separately, consistency of the whole decision making process becomes a crucial issue. This is the main motivation of the integrated model to be presented later.

*

*   *

Chapter II

Job-Shop Sequencing and Scheduling

II.1   Introduction

In the framework of the integrated model introduced in Chapter III, we are first interested in finding an optimal schedule in a **job-shop**. This difficult problem has been largely discussed in the literature for more than 20 years (see [Balas 69], [Mc Mahon et Florian 75], [Baker 87], [Carlier 78], [Lageweg *et al.* 77], [Barker and Mc Mahon 85] or [Carlier and Pinson 89]), and still remains a major problem in combinatorial optimization. In the general case, it has been shown to be $\mathcal{NP}$-hard (see [Rinnooy Kan 76] for instance).

After a survey of the various methodologies for the job-shop scheduling problem, we will discuss more extensively the two heuristic methods that we use, namely the shifting bottleneck procedure ([Adams *et al.* 88]), and a priority rule-based dispatching heuristic (see [Conway *et al.* 67]).

An exact method is not suitable for our purpose. Indeed, in the iterative method to be presented in Chapter III, we have to solve a scheduling problem at each iteration, so that we need a method that can solve medium size problems in a reasonable amount of time.

The shifting bottleneck procedure is convenient because it finds *good* solutions relatively fast. This is true if we only consider the *simplest* version of the procedure, and not the enumerative version (see [Adams *et al.* 88]).

The priority rule-based dispatching heuristic has been implemented in order to observe the impact of the scheduling algorithm efficiency on our iterative planning and scheduling procedure. Moreover, when running the iterative planning procedure on large size examples, this simple and very fast heuristic is needed.

When implementing the shifting bottleneck procedure, several of its drawbacks appeared. Thus, we propose a modified version ([Dauzere-Peres and Lasserre 93]), based on a new algorithm for the one-machine sequencing problem with general dependencies ([Dauzere-Peres 90]).

Even if a large part of this work is devoted to the general job-shop scheduling problem:

- the main goal is to integrate scheduling (actually sequencing) constraints in the computation of the production plan, in order for this plan to be *feasible*.

- our integrated model and the associated iterative procedure, remain valid for a large number of workshops (flow-shop, open-shop, ...), and can be extended to various special cases (no work-in-process inventories, ...).

II.2   Job-Shop Scheduling

II.2.1   Definitions

In the general job-shop scheduling problem, n jobs have to be sequenced on m machines. The sequence of machines (routing) on which a job has to be processed is fixed, and each machine can only process one job at a time.

The following notation is used:

$J = \{J_1, J_2, .., J_n\}$ is the set of jobs.
$M = \{1, .., m\}$ is the set of machines.
o_{ijk} is the jth operation on the routing of job J_i, which has to be processed on machine $k \in M$.
r_i and d_i are the release date and the due date of job J_i, respectively.
t_{ijk}, r_{ijk} and p_{ijk} are the start time, the release date and the processing time of operation o_{ijk}, respectively.
C_i is the completion time of job J_i.
$L_i = C_i - d_i$ is the lateness, and $T_i = \max(0, L_i)$ the tardiness of job J_i.

No preemption is allowed, *i.e.*, every operation, once started, cannot be interrupted. The routing can vary from one job to another. The problem is to determine a sequence of jobs on each machine so that the maximum completion time $C_{max} = \max_{J_i \in J} C_i$, often called the *makespan*, is minimized. This problem is denoted as $J| |C_{max}$ (see Chapter I, and the classification introduced in [Lawler *et al.* 93]). Other criteria can be considered (*e.g.*, sum of the completion times, lateness, ...). As we shall see in Chapter III, the problem of minimizing the makespan is of interest for us, because minimizing the maximum lateness reduces to minimizing the makespan on a related problem.

A very interesting representation of $J| |C_{max}$ is provided by using a disjunctive graph (see [Roy and Sussman 64] and [Balas 69]) $G = (N, A, E)$. N is the set of nodes in the graph (all the operations plus dummy start and finish operations 0 and $*$). A is the set of conjunctive arcs, and E the set of disjunctive arcs.

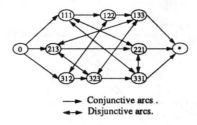

Figure II-1: Disjunctive graph.

As shown in the example of Figure II-1, the conjunctive arcs model the precedence constraints in the routings of the jobs, and the disjunctive arcs model the machine utilization. A disjunctive arc is set between every pair of operations that must be processed on the same machine. For example, operations o_{111}, o_{221}, and o_{331} have to be performed on machine 1.

E can be divided into subsets E_k. E_k corresponds to a set of disjunctive arcs associated to the machine k, and $E = \bigcup_{k \in M} E_k$.

To each conjunctive arc between two operations is associated a length equal to the processing time of the operation from which the arc is starting.

A **selection** S_k in E_k corresponds to the choice of a conjunctive arc (*i.e.*, of a direction) for each disjunctive arc in E_k. A selection is called *acyclic* if it has no directed cycle. A **complete** selection S consists of the union of selections S_k, one in each E_k, $k \in M$.

Sequencing the jobs on the machines means choosing an acyclic complete selection S in E. $G_S = (N, A, S)$ denotes the directed graph associated to the sequence.

The scheduling problem can be written:

$$
O \begin{cases}
\min t_* & \\
t_{ijk} - t_{ij'k'} \geq p_{ij'k'} & \forall (o_{ij'k'}, o_{ijk}) \in A \\
t_{ijk} \geq 0 & \forall o_{ijk} \in N \\
t_{ijk} - t_{i'j'k} \geq p_{i'j'k} \; or \; t_{i'j'k} - t_{ijk} \geq p_{ijk} & \forall (o_{i'j'k}, o_{jk}) \in E_k, \; k \in M
\end{cases}
$$

A solution of (O) is called a **schedule**, *i.e.*, a *sequence* and a choice of start times for each operation. The solution set of (O) is generally *infinite*. However, to each schedule is associated one and only one sequence (acyclic complete selection) in the set of sequences which is *finite*.

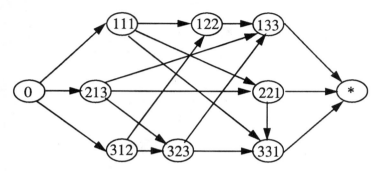

Figure II-2: Graph with choice of a complete selection.

Looking back at the example in Figure II-1, with the complete selection represented in Figure II-2, one can create, for instance, the two schedules depicted in the Gantt chart in Figure II-3, and vice-versa.

Solving $J| |C_{max}$ is determining a sequence (acyclic complete selection S) which minimizes the length of the longest path.

For each selection S, there exists a schedule which minimizes every criterion in the set of schedules associated to S. This schedule, called *semi-active*, is created by shifting all the operations as much as possible to the left, *i.e.*, by starting the operation immediately after the completion of the previous operation in the routing or on the same machine. In the previous example, only the first schedule in Figure II-3 is semi-active.

One may distinguish two subsets in the *finite* set of semi-active schedules:

1. the set of *nondelay* schedules in which a machine cannot remain idle if some operation is ready for processing.

2. the set of *active* schedules (which contains the set of nondelay schedules) in which a machine may remain idle and wait for an operation o_{ijk} even if some operations are ready for immediate processing (*schedulable*). However, the waiting time cannot be larger than the processing time of a schedulable operation $o_{i'j'k}$, since $o_{i'j'k}$ could be processed without changing the start time of o_{ijk}.

As already noted in Chapter I, two kinds of methods have been developed to solve scheduling problems: **exact methods** determine an *optimal* solution to the

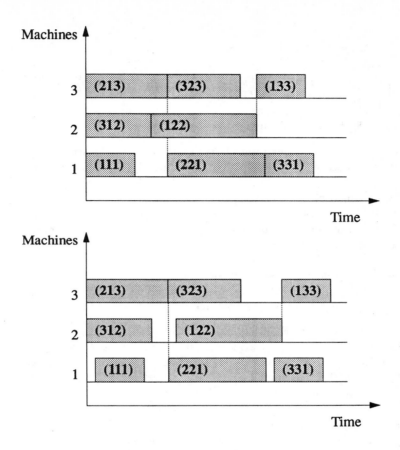

Figure II-3: Gantt charts.

problem, whereas **approximate methods**, or **heuristics**, do not ensure optimality of the solution but require much smaller computing times.

In the following sections, several methods for solving the job-shop scheduling problem are reviewed.

II.2.2   Exact Methods

The first method consists in transforming the scheduling problem (O) into a mixed-integer linear programming problem. Each disjunction on a pair $(o_{ijk}, o_{i'j'k})$ of operations is modeled by using two constraints and a Boolean variable $y_{ijk,i'j'k}$.

(O) becomes:

$$O' \begin{cases} t_{ijk} - t_{ij'k'} \geq p_{ij'k'} & \forall (o_{ij'k'}, o_{ijk}) \in A \\ t_{ijk} \geq 0 & \forall o_{ijk} \in N \\ t_{ijk} - t_{i'j'k} \geq p_{i'j'k} - B.y_{ijk,i'j'k} & \forall (o_{i'j'k}, o_{ijk}) \in E_k, \ k \in M \quad (1) \\ t_{i'j'k} - t_{ijk} \geq p_{ijk} - B.(1 - y_{ijk,i'j'k}) & \forall (o_{i'j'k}, o_{ijk}) \in E_k, \ k \in M \quad (2) \end{cases}$$

where B is chosen big enough.

If $y_{ijk,i'j'k} = 1$, then Constraint (1) is redundant, and Constraint (2) states that operation o_{ijk} precedes operation $o_{i'j'k}$. Similarly, $y_{ijk,i'j'k} = 0$ implies that $o_{i'j'k}$ precedes o_{ijk}.

Thus, solving (O'), $i.e.$, choosing a value for each Boolean variable, means solving every conflict on the machines. However, the complexity of the problem remains the same. The computing time to solve this mixed-integer linear programming model grows exponentially with the problem size, and is already very large even for very small size problems. In particular, when relaxing the integer constraints in (O'), the B coefficient induces very poor lower bounds.

Other formulations of (O) as a mixed-integer linear programming problem are possible, but without significant advantage.

The most efficient methods for this kind of problems seem to be *Branch and Bound* procedures. The set of all the possible solutions is considered, so that an optimal solution will eventually be found. But, with a *clever* exploration of this set, $i.e.$, with an effective branching and a good evaluation, the search is shortened because large parts of the solution set, in which no optimal solution can be found, are not explored.

Therefore, computing a good lower bound at each node of the tree search is essential. In [Bratley et al. 73], the lower bound is computed by solving the scheduling problem on one machine. This idea has initiated a lot of research on the one-machine scheduling problem with the maximum lateness criterion (or an equivalent problem with the makespan criterion).

[Giffler and Thompson 60] first proposed the enumeration scheme which consists of generating all the active schedules, since the optimal solution is in the set of active schedules ([Conway et $al.$ 67]). At each step, N', the subset of operations whose predecessors have been scheduled, is computed, as well as the the earliest date $(r_{ijk} + p_{ijk})$ at which each operation can be completed. Then, it suffices to consider the machine on which this date is minimal, and to create as many branches as operations with release date lower than this minimum.

[Balas 69] is one of the first to propose a procedure which implicitly enumerates feasible ($i.e.$, acyclic) graphs. This procedure is based on the fact that every conjunctive graph $G_{S'}$, created by reversing a disjunctive arc on a critical path of a feasible conjunctive graph G_S, is also feasible. Therefore, if the length of critical paths of a graph $G_{S'}$ is lower than in G_S, then at least one disjunctive arc of one of the critical paths in G_S is inverted in $G_{S'}$.

[Carlier and Pinson 89] propose an original procedure, also based on a disjunctive graph modeling. Using this procedure, they were the first to prove that 930 is actually the minimum makespan of the famous 10 jobs and 10 machines (10×10) problem given in [Fisher and Thompson 63].

Finally, [Brucker 91] presents a method that solves the 10x10 problem in the shortest computing time reported so far, 16 minutes on a workstation.

Despite recent improvements, these methods are far from being able to solve large size problems yet. This is why numerous approximate methods have been, and still are, extensively studied to solve realistic size problems.

II.2.3   Heuristic Procedures

In practice, heuristics are the only tools to tackle actual size problems that exact methods cannot handle up to now.

II.2.3.1   List Scheduling Algorithms

A large majority of heuristics uses list scheduling. Starting from some initial time, operations are sequenced on the machines according to given priority rules (sometimes dynamic), and the availability of the machines.

An active schedule is generated as in the procedure of [Giffler and Thompson 60] discussed in the previous section. But, at each step, only one branch (a single operation) is selected, depending on the chosen priority rule.

Based on many experimentations, [Conway *et al.* 67] note that generating only nondelay schedules with priority rules, seems to be as efficient (if not more efficient) as generating active schedules.

Most of the comparative studies (see for instance [Conway *et al.* 67], [Adams *et al.* 88] or [Montazeri and Van Wassenhove 90]) of various priority rules show a large diversity in the solutions. According to the sample and the criterion, the quality of a rule can change a lot. In general, it is difficult to claim that a rule dominates the others.

The priority rules that we have chosen in later chapters, and the details of the algorithm used to generate schedules are presented in Section II.5.

II.2.3.2   Other Methods

Another method to build a solution for a scheduling problem is to successively sequence — *i.e.*, determine the ordering of operations — the machines one after the other.

The most well-known procedure of this kind is the shifting bottleneck procedure proposed by [Adams *et al.* 88]. This procedure is detailed in the following sections, and we propose a modified version to eliminate some of its drawbacks.

Other methods are based on local search algorithms.

Once a notion of neighborhood has been defined, a simple local search algorithm can be written as in ([Carlier and Chrétienne 88]):

1. Find an initial solution x.

2. Among the z neighbors of x, determine one which minimizes $f(z)$.

3. If $f(z) < f(x)$, replace x by z and go to 2. Otherwise, keep x as the best solution.

with f being a function which evaluates the cost associated to each solution.

More sophisticated local search algorithms are:

- *Simulated Annealing* ([Van Laarhoven *et al.* 92]) in which, at every step k, a neighbor is chosen randomly. If the cost is decreasing, this neighbor is visited, otherwise it is visited with a probability which decreases with k according to a given (cooling) law. Under some assumptions, convergence *in probability* to a global optimum is ensured.

- *Taboo search* (see [Taillard 89]) temporarily prevents moves already made in order to avoid cycles.

The primary interesting factor in these algorithms is that they are general purpose methods, easily implementable. Moreover, good numerical results are reported, but the computing time required to obtain such results remains prohibitive, and prevents these methods from being used in our framework, developed in later chapters.

II.3   The Shifting Bottleneck Procedure

II.3.1   Introduction

In this section, we detail the *Shifting Bottleneck* (SB) *procedure* [Adams *et al.* 88], for the job-shop scheduling problem with the makespan criterion. This procedure is known to outperform most of the other heuristics, both in terms of performance and computing times (see [Lawler *et al.* 93], and the comparative study in [Adams *et al.* 88]).

This procedure consists of solving successive **One-Machine Sequencing** (OMS) **problems** with an algorithm proposed by [Carlier 82], closely related to the one by

[Mc Mahon and Florian 75], and very efficient in practice. Let M be the set of all machines, and M_0 the set of machines already sequenced. At each step of the procedure, the most critical machine, so-called **bottleneck machine**, is selected by solving an OMS problem on each machine not yet sequenced (*i.e.*, in the set M/M_0) and included into M_0. In addition, on each machine in M_0, the sequence is re-optimized, again using Carlier's algorithm. Finally, the same is done on machines which are on the critical path. Despite good performances in practice, this procedure has some drawbacks. To eliminate these drawbacks, discussed at the end of this section, a modified version is proposed in Section II.4.

The Shifting Bottleneck procedure is described in details in the sequel, as it can be found in [Adams *et al.* 88] and [Carlier 82], in order to explain later our modifications.

II.3.2 The Shifting Bottleneck Procedure

The machines are considered successively one by one, in an OMS problem, and the result is used to both rank the machines, and select an optimal sequence on the machine with highest rank. This machine is added to the set of machines already sequenced. Then, the makespan may be improved by solving again OMS problems in this set.

Let M_0 be the set of machines that have been already sequenced, by choosing selections S_k ($k \in M_0$). Let $O(l, M_0)$ be the problem obtained by replacing each arc set E_k ($k \in M_0$) with the corresponding selection S_k, and deleting each arc set E_k ($k \in M \backslash M_0 \backslash \{l\}$).

$O(l, M_0)$ is an OMS problem:

$$O(l, M_0) \begin{cases} v(l, M_0) = \min\ t_* \\ t_{ijk} - t_{ij'k'} \geq p_{ij'k'} & \forall (o_{ij'k'}, o_{ijk}) \in A \\ t_{ijk} \geq 0 & \forall o_{ijk} \in N \\ t_{ijk} - t_{i'j'k} \geq p_{i'j'k} & \forall (o_{i'j'k}, o_{ijk}) \in S_k,\ k \in M_0 \\ t_{ijl} - t_{i'j'l} \geq p_{i'j'l}\ or\ t_{i'j'l} - t_{ijl} \geq p_{ijl} & \forall (o_{i'j'l}, o_{ijl}) \in E_l \end{cases}$$

A **bottleneck** machine $k_g \in M \backslash M_0$ is such that:

$$v(k_g, M_0) = \max\{v(k, M_0) : k \in M \backslash M_0\}$$

where $v(k, M_0)$ is the optimal solution of $O(k, M_0)$.

Therefore, the SB procedure is as follows:

Start with $M_0 := \phi$.

1. **Identify** *the bottleneck machine* k_g *among machines* $k \in M \backslash M_0$ *and its optimal sequence (selection* S_{k_g}*).* $M_0 \leftarrow M_0 \cup \{k_g\}$*. Go to 2.*

2. **Re-optimize** *successively the sequence of each critical machine* $k \in M_0$*, i.e.: set* $M'_0 = M_0 \backslash \{k\}$ *and solve* $O(k, M'_0)$*. If* $M_0 = M$*, STOP; otherwise go to 1.*

The result of the OMS problem will be used to both determine the *bottleneck* machine and an optimal *sequence* for this machine.

$l(o_{ijk}, o_{i'j'k'})$ is defined as the length of the longest path between operations o_{ijk} and $o_{i'j'k'}$. $r_{ijk} = l(0, o_{ijk})$ is the *release date* of operation o_{ijk}, and $q_{ijk} = l(o_{ijk}, *) - p_{ijk}$ the *delivery time, i.e.,* the minimum amount of time to be spent in the system after the end of operation o_{ijk}.

Then, $O(k, M_0)$ can be written:

$$O(k, M_0) \begin{cases} \min t_* \\ t_{ijk} \geq r_{ijk} & \forall o_{ijk} \in N \\ t_* - t_{ijk} \geq q_{ijk} + p_{ijk} & \forall o_{ijk} \in N \\ t_{ijk} - t_{i'j'k} \geq p_{i'j'k} \ or \ t_{i'j'k} - t_{ijk} \geq p_{ijk} & \forall (o_{i'j'k}, o_{ijk}) \in E_k \end{cases}$$

This problem is solved by applying Carlier's algorithm. This algorithm is also used in Step 2 of the procedure, called **local re-optimization procedure** in [Adams *et al.* 88] and described below.

Let $k_1, k_2, ..., k_l$ be an ordering of M_0 ($l =| M_0 |$). The **local re-optimization cycle** is:

for $i = 1$ *to* l*, solve problem* $O(k_i, M_0 \backslash \{k_i\})$ *and substitute the optimal selection* S_{k_i} *to the old selection.*

As long as $| M_0 | < | M |$, at most three local re-optimization cycles are processed. Note that the number three is arbitrary. Indeed, the SB procedure is *sensitive* to this parameter as observed on some examples where increasing this value leads to an *erratic* behavior of the makespan. At the last step, the local re-optimization is done until no improvement is achieved in a full cycle.

Before each cycle, the elements of M_0 are reordered according to the decreasing values of the solutions of $O(k_i, M_0 \backslash \{k_i\})$.

Finally, it has been found useful to repeat this procedure after temporarily removing from the problem the last α non-critical machines (where α is the minimum between $| M_0 |^{1/2}$ and the number of noncritical machines in M_0). In [Adams *et al.* 88], nothing is really explained about how to re-introduce the α removed machines except that they must be re-introduced successively. So, we have tested different strategies and decided to keep the best, even if it is the most time consuming, *i.e.,* each time a machine is re-introduced, the local re-optimization procedure is repeated.

II.3.3 The One-Machine Sequencing Problem

II.3.3.1 Introduction

The One-Machine Sequencing (OMS) problem with release dates r_i, processing times p_i, and due dates d_i has been extensively studied in the literature. Although [Lenstra *et al.* 77] showed that the general $1/r_j/L_{max}$ problem (where L_{max} is the maximum lateness) is strongly $\mathcal{NP}$-hard, some special cases such as $1/pmtn, r_j/L_{max}$ ([Horn 74]) and $1/r_j, p_j = p/L_{max}$ ([Garey *et al.* 81]) can be solved with polynomial-time algorithms, and remain well solved when precedence constraints arise.

Various enumerative methods exist for solving $1/prec, r_j/L_{max}$. One approach is proposed by [Mc Mahon and Florian 75], improved by [Lageweg *et al.* 77] who replace due dates with *delivery times* q_i, and [Carlier 82] who presents one of the most efficient algorithms for this problem. Besides, [Zdrzalka and Grabowski 89] consider extensions of these methods to $1/prec, r_j/f_{max}$ (where $f_{max} \in \{C_{max}, L_{max}\}$).

In the remaining of this section, we describe Carlier's algorithm, extensively used in the Shifting Bottleneck (SB) procedure. Then, an algorithm is proposed to take into account the new precedence constraints induced by the SB procedure.

The problem is to minimize the makespan of jobs that must be processed on a single machine. J^* denotes the set of these jobs. For each job J_i, p_i, r_i, t_i, and q_i denote the processing time, release date, start time, and delivery time respectively.

With this notation, $O(k, M_0)$ is stated as:

$$\begin{cases} \min \ C_{max} \\ t_i \geq r_i & \forall J_i \in J^* \\ C_{max} - t_i \geq q_i + p_i & \forall J_i \in J^* \\ t_i - t_j \geq p_j \ or \ t_j - t_i \geq p_i & \forall (J_j, J_i) \in J^* \times J^*, J_i \neq J_j \end{cases}$$

II.3.3.2 Carlier's Algorithm

It is a *Branch and Bound* procedure where each node is evaluated by using Schrage's algorithm.

Schrage's algorithm:

> U *is the set of jobs already scheduled.*
> $\overline{U}$ *is the set of all other jobs.*

> 1. *Set* $t := \min_{J_i \in J^*} r_i$, $U := \phi$
>
> 2. *At time* t, *schedule among "ready" jobs* J_i $(r_i \leq t)$ *of* $\overline{U}$, *the job* J_j *with the greatest* q_i.
>
> 3. *Set* $U := U \bigcup \{J_j\}$; $t_j := t$; $t := \max(t_j + p_j, \min_{J_i \in \overline{U}} r_i)$.
>   *If* U *is equal to* J^*, *STOP; otherwise go to 2.*

Carlier's procedure is based on this algorithm and on the following theorem.

Theorem II.1

Let C_{max} be the makespan of Schrage's schedule.
*If the schedule is **not** optimal, there is a critical job J_c and a critical set I $(I \subset J^*)$*
such that:

$$h_J = \min_{J_i \in I} r_i + \sum_{J_i \in I} p_i + \min_{J_i \in I} q_i > C_{max} - p_c$$

Consequently, the distance to the optimum from Schrage's schedule is less than p_c; moreover, in an optimal schedule, either J_c will be processed before all jobs of I, or J_c will be processed after all jobs of I.

See a proof in [Carlier 82].

Le us number the jobs in the ordering of Schrage's sequence. If c exists, it is the greatest subscript in a critical path $[J_1, .., J_p]$ such that $q_c < q_p$, and $I = [J_{c+1}, .., J_p]$.

Carlier's algorithm:

Each node v of the tree is associated to a one-machine problem with a lower bound f_v (f is the value of the current lower bound). The upper bound f^{sup} is the value of the best solution known so far.
$V =$set of nodes.

Initialization:

$V := \phi$ and $v := 0$.
Apply Schrage's algorithm and compute the makespan C_{max}.
Search for J_c and I.
$f_0 := h_I$. $f := f_0$. $f^{sup} := C_{max}$.

While J_c exists,

1. *Consider two new problems, one in which J_c has to be processed before all jobs of I by setting:*

$$q_c := \max(q_c, \sum_{J_r \in I} p_r + q_p);$$

   and another in which J_c has to be processed after all jobs of I by setting:

$$r_c := \max(r_c, \min_{J_r \in I} r_r + \sum_{J_r \in I} p_r).$$

   For each problem, the lower bound $f_\beta := \max(f, h_{I \bigcup \{J_c\}})$ is computed, and a new node β is added to V (with its lower bound f_β) if $f_\beta < f^{sup}$.

2. $J_c = 0$. $f_v = 0$.
   While (J_c does not exist) and ($V \neq \phi$) and ($f^{sup} > f_v$), search in V for the node v with the lowest bound, remove v from N, apply Schrage's algorithm and search for J_c, I and f ($f = \max(f_v, h_I)$).

$h_{I \bigcup \{J_c\}}$ is computed with the modified r_c or q_c. After each run of Schrage's algorithm, the solution is stored if less than f^{sup}.

The algorithm eventually stops in a node, *i.e.*, an optimal solution has been found **for this node**, if the following proposition holds.

Proposition II.1
Let y be a sequence determined with Schrage's algorithm. If y has a critical path $IC = [J_{i_1}, .., J_{i_p}]$ such that:

$$\forall J_j \in IC \backslash \{J_{i_p}\} \qquad q_j \geq q_{i_p}$$

then, this schedule is optimal.

This method gives an optimal solution, with very good computing times, until 1000 jobs. Moreover, the extension to include precedence constraints of the form $t_j - t_i \geq p_i$ is known to be straightforward (see [Lageweg *et al.* 77]). It suffices to update release dates and delivery times such that $r_j \geq r_i + p_j$ and $q_i \geq q_j + p_j$, whenever J_i precedes J_j.

Let us take a simple example which will be useful in the sequel.

Example II.1
We consider 6 jobs with the following data:

Jobs	J_1	J_2	J_3	J_4	J_5	J_6
Release dates	*0*	*2*	*5*	*8*	*10*	*15*
Processing times	*4*	*4*	*2*	*1*	*3*	*2*
Delivery times	*9*	*10*	*13*	*6*	*7*	*6*

Schrage's algorithm gives the sequence $(J_1, J_2, J_3, J_5, J_4, J_6)$ with a makespan of $C_{max} = 23$, which is optimal because $C_{max} = r_6 + p_6 + q_6$.

II.3.4 Remarks on the Shifting Bottleneck Procedure

The SB procedure extensively uses Carlier's algorithm in which the jobs are treated as **independent** whereas, in OMS problems of the SB procedure, some jobs may be **dependent**, *i.e.*, in the graph, there might exist a path between two jobs of a machine to be sequenced. This path is generated by the sequences of other machines already sequenced. As shown later in Section II.4.1, the straightforward extension of Carlier's algorithm to simple precedence constraints is not valid.

Hence, when OMS problems are solved, the makespan may be *underestimated*. Therefore, it is sometimes impossible to find an optimal sequence with Carlier's algorithm and, in the first step of the SB procedure, an incorrect bottleneck machine may be selected. Moreover, in the re-optimization step, the makespan may increase. Augmenting the number of local re-optimization cycles often leads to an erratic behavior of the makespan, and for instance, the final result is totally different when one switches from three to four cycles.

II.4   A   Modified   Shifting   Bottleneck   Procedure

II.4.1   Drawbacks of the Shifting Bottleneck Procedure

The disjunctive graph of Figure II-4 represents a job-shop scheduling problem with 5 jobs and 4 machines.

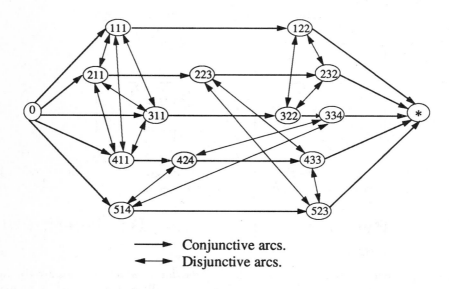

⟶ Conjunctive arcs.
⟷ Disjunctive arcs.

Figure II-4: Disjunctive graph.

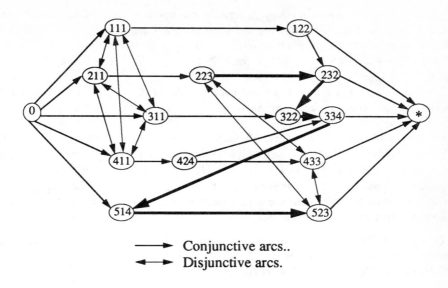

                    ⟶ Conjunctive arcs..
                    ⟷ Disjunctive arcs.

Figure II-5: Disjunctive graph with selections S_2 and S_4.

In the graph of Figure II-5, with machines 2 and 4 already sequenced (selections S_2 and S_4), jobs 2 and 5 are not *independent* since there is a *path* between operations o_{223} and o_{523} (path o_{223}; o_{232}; o_{322}; o_{334}; o_{514}; o_{523}), and thus the start time of o_{523} depends on the start time of o_{223}: $t_{523} \geq t_{223} + p_{223} + p_{232} + p_{322} + p_{334} + p_{514}$. In other words, if one has to sequence jobs J_2, J_4 and J_5 on machine 3, the schedule must be such that J_5 is processed after J_2, and their start times must verify the previous relation.

The length of the longest path between dependent operations is called the **minimal duration** between their start times. In the literature on one-machine problems, some methods take account of possible precedence constraints (see Section II.3.3) of the form $t_j - t_i \geq p_i$ if J_i precedes J_j. But we want to consider more general precedence constraints of the form $t_j - t_i \geq p_{ij}$, where p_{ij} can be greater than p_i.

Let J_i and J_j be two dependent jobs, let r_i and r_j be their release dates, p_{ij} the *minimal duration* between the beginning of J_i and J_j, and $r_j = p_{ij} + r_i$. If in a schedule, $t_i > r_i$, then the *true* release date of J_j is $r'_j := p_{ij} + t_i > r_j$. But, there is no algorithm for OMS problems in which the value r_j is updated when t_i is known, and therefore, the makespan computed could be **lower** than the real one.

Let us illustrate this point with the problem given in Example II.1.

Example II.2
Let $p_{35} = 5$ be the minimal duration between the start times of J_3 and J_5. Th

release dates and delivery times of J_3 and J_5 are updated since $r_5 = r_3 + p_{35}$ and $q_3 = q_5 + p_{35} - p_3 + p_5$. The sequence determined with Carlier's algorithm is the one given in Example II.1 with start times ($t_1 = 0$, $t_2 = 4$, $t_3 = 8$, $t_5 = 10$, $t_4 = 13$, $t_6 = 15$), and $C_{max} = 23$. In fact, since $t_5 \geq t_3 + p_{35}$, the actual value of t_5 is 13, then $t_4 = 16$, $t_6 = 17$ and $C_{max} = 25$.

Moreover, one can see that the sequence ($J_1, J_2, J_3, J_4, J_5, J_6$), which cannot be determined by Carlier's algorithm, has a lower makespan $C_{max} = 24$.

At Step 2 of the SB procedure, let C_{max} be the makespan obtained by solving $O(k(i), M_0 \backslash \{k(i)\})$ (selection $S'_{k(i)}$) with selections $S_{k(1)}, \ldots, S_{k(i-1)}, S_{k(i+1)}, \ldots, S_{k(p)}$. When, in the next iteration, $O(k(i+1), M_0 \backslash \{k(i+1)\})$ is solved (selection $S'_{k(i+1)}$), the new makespan C'_{max} is sometimes larger than C_{max}. If $O(k(i+1), M_0 \backslash \{k(i+1)\})$ was solved optimally, this increase would not happen since one can find a selection at least as good as S_{i+1}, because S_{i+1} would again give C_{max}.

Our goal is to take the dependencies between jobs into account in the algorithm, in order to obtain better results in the local re-optimization procedure, and to eliminate the last part of this procedure.

The value p_{ij} has the following properties :

1. $p_{ij} = p_{ji} = 0 \Leftrightarrow J_i$ and J_j are independent.

2. $p_{ij} \neq 0 \Leftrightarrow J_i$ is before $J_j \Rightarrow p_{ji} = 0$

3. $p_{ij} \neq 0$ and $p_{jk} \neq 0 \Rightarrow p_{ik} \neq 0$

4. $p_{ij} \neq 0 \Rightarrow r_j \geq r_i + p_{ij}$

The OMS problem with dependent jobs can be stated as:

$$\begin{cases} \min C_{max} \\ t_i \geq r_i & \forall J_i \in J^* \\ C_{max} - t_i \geq q_i + p_i & \forall J_i \in J^* \\ t_i - t_j \geq p_j \text{ or } t_j - t_i \geq p_i & \forall (J_j, J_i) \in J^* \times J^*, J_i \neq J_j \\ t_j - t_i \geq p_{ij} & \forall (J_j, J_i) \in J^* \times J^*, J_i \neq J_j \text{ and such that } p_{ij} \neq 0 \end{cases}$$

To take the new inequalities into account in Carlier's algorithm, our modifications consist of:

- **updating** the release dates of the jobs each time we choose one in Schrage's algorithm.

- trying to **decrease** the modified release dates of dependent jobs which are on a critical path.

II.4.2 The Dependent Job Algorithm

Our first modification is made in Schrage's algorithm where, each time a job J_i is added to the sequence (so that its start time is known), we update the release date of one or more jobs among the jobs not yet chosen.

The Modified Schrage algorithm.

U *set of jobs already scheduled.*
$\overline{U}$ *set of all other jobs.*
$p_{ij}(J_i, J_j \in J^*)$ *minimal duration between J_i and J_j.*

1. *Set* $t := \min\limits_{J_i \in J^*} r_i,\ U := \phi.$

2. *At time t, schedule among "ready" jobs J_i ($r_i \le t$) of $\overline{U}$, the job J_j with the greatest q_i.*

3. *Set $U := U \bigcup \{J_j\}$;*
   for all $J_i \in \overline{U}$, **if** $(p_{ji} \neq 0)$ **and** $(r_i < t + p_{ji})$ **then** $r_i := t + p_{ji}$
   $t_j := t.\ t := \max(t_j + p_j, \min\limits_{J_i \in \overline{U}} r_i).$
   If U is equal to J^*, then $STOP$; otherwise, go to 2.

Dependent jobs are updated in Step 3. Now, in Step 2, we guarantee to choose a **real** "ready" job and not one with an underestimated release date. Looking at Example II.2, this modification prevents us from computing the sequence with $C_{max} = 25$, and enables us to find the one with $C_{max} = 24$.

A critical path $IC = [J_{i_1}, .., J_{i_p}]$ in a sequence determined by the modified Schrage algorithm is the path with the longest length equal to the makespan $C_{max} = r'_{i_1} + \sum\limits_{J_{i_k} \in IC} p_{i_k} + q_{i_p}$ (where r'_{i_1} denotes the release date of J_{i_1} after the modified Schrage algorithm).

It appears that the release date r_j of a job J_j can depend on the start time t_i of another job J_i. To decrease the makespan, it is interesting to decrease t_i, and then perhaps t_j, if J_j is on a critical path. Necessary conditions can be deduced.

Necessary conditions:

Let r_k, r'_k ($J_k \in J^*$) be the values of the release dates respectively before and after the modified Schrage algorithm. To be able to reduce the release date of a job on a critical path in reducing t_i, J_i must satisfy the following conditions:

i). $p_{ij} \neq 0$ and $r'_j = t_i + p_{ij}$
ii). $r'_j \neq r_j$
iii). job J_j on a critical path

Condition $i)$ just states the dependence of J_i and J_j. Condition $ii)$ ensures that a decrease of t_i will reduce the release date of J_j (and also ensures that $t_i > r_i$). If Condition $iii)$ is not satisfied, there is no advantage in reducing r'_j, $i.e.$, reducing t_i.

Our problem is now, **in Carlier's algorithm, how to decrease** t_i, **if job** J_i **satisfies these conditions?**

We consider J_i as the end of **an artificial critical path**. The latter is defined as the longest path $IC' = [J_l, .., J_i]$ ended by J_i $(S_i = r'_l + \sum\limits_{J_k \in IC' \backslash \{J_i\}} p_k)$, and such that J_i verifies the necessary conditions with a job either on a *real* critical path, or on another *artificial* critical path.

Then, we use the following proposition.

Proposition II.2
Let S be a modified Schrage's schedule, and let J_{i_p} be the end of an artificial *critical path $IC' = [J_{i_1}, .., J_{i_p}]$. The start time t_{i_p} can be reduced, without increasing the makespan, only if there is:*

1. *A job $J_{i_l} \in [J_{i_1}, .., J_{i_{p-1}}]$ such that $p_{i_l i_p} = 0$ and $q_{i_l} + p_{i_l} < C_{max} - r_{i_p} - p_{i_p}$, or*

2. *A job J_k which verifies the necessary conditions with a job in IC', and such that its start time can be reduced (i.e., condition 1 or condition 2 is verified for J_k).*

In the first case, J_{i_l} is moved after J_{i_p}. In the second, t_k is decreased and the modified Schrage algorithm is applied.

Proof:
1. $t_{i_p} = r_{i_1} + \sum_{k=1}^{p-1} p_{i_k}$. Obviously, if a job J_{i_l} is moved after J_{i_p}, this value will decrease. However, J_{i_l} and J_{i_p} must be independent $(p_{i_l i_p} = 0)$. Now, suppose that J_{i_l} is after J_{i_p} in a schedule and that $q_{i_l} + p_{i_l} \geq C_{max} - r_{i_p} - p_{i_p}$. The length of the path $[J_{i_p}, .., J_{i_l}]$ is greater than or equal to:

$$t_{i_p} + p_{i_p} + p_{i_l} + q_{i_l} \geq t_{i_p} + p_{i_p} + p_{i_l} + C_{max} - r_{i_p} - p_{i_p} - p_{i_l} = t_{i_p} + C_{max} - r_{i_p}$$

$$\Rightarrow \quad t_{i_p} + p_{i_p} + p_{i_l} + q_{i_l} \geq C_{max}$$

because $t_{i_p} \geq r_{i_p}$. Then the makespan of this schedule could never be lower than C_{max}.

2. Except condition 1, the only way to decrease t_{i_p} in one Schrage schedule is to change the critical path, $i.e.$, reduce the release dates of jobs on IC'. ♣

Because of Condition 2 in the previous proposition, we are going to search for new *artificial* critical paths. This procedure will be repeated until no more critical path is added.

In the branch and bound method, we will search for the **first** *artificial* critical path IC' (*i.e.*, whose last job is sequenced before the last jobs of other *artificial* critical paths) where condition 1 is verified. If this path exists, we know that condition 2 is not verified because there would be another *artificial* critical path before IC', in which condition 1 would be verified.

As in Carlier's algorithm and for a *real* critical path, two nodes will be created for the job J_{i_l} which verifies condition 1, and with the largest subscript ($l \geq k$, $\forall J_{i_k}$ verifying condition 1). Note that $p_{i_l i_k} = 0$ ($\forall J_{i_k} \in [J_{i_{l+1}}, .., J_{i_{p-1}}]$), otherwise the job J_{i_k} for which $p_{i_l i_k} \neq 0$ would also verify condition 1, and with a larger subscript.

In the first node, J_{i_l} will stay before J_{i_p}, but not always before $[J_{i_{l+1}}, .., J_{i_{p-1}}]$ since the theorem is no longer valid. Therefore, q_{i_l} cannot be increased as in Carlier's algorithm. Instead, $p_{i_l i_p}$ will be set to p_{i_l} to create a precedence relation between J_{i_l} and J_{i_p}. J_{i_l} will be processed after J_{i_p} in the second node. However, every job in $[J_{i_{l+1}}, .., J_{i_{p-1}}]$ does not verify condition 1 and therefore has to be processed before J_{i_p}. Hence, J_{i_l} must be set after all jobs of $J = [J_{i_{l+1}}, .., J_{i_p}]$. As previously, the minimal durations $p_{i_k i_l}$ ($\forall J_{i_k} \in J$) will be set to p_{i_k}.

This modification is illustrated on the following example.

Example II.3

The data are given in Example II.1. As we previously saw, the modified Schrage algorithm gives a makespan of 24 with the sequence $(J_1, J_2, J_3, J_4, J_5, J_6)$. Since J_3 verifies the necessary conditions (i.e., $p_{35} \neq 0$, $r'_5 = S_3 + p_{35}$, $r'_5 \neq r_5$ and J_5 is on the critical path), it is the end of an artificial critical path. Then, a sequence will be created in which J_2 will be processed after J_3 $(J_1, J_3, J_2, J_5, J_4, J_6)$, because $q_2 + p_2 < 24 - r_3 - p_3$, with $C_{max} = 23$ which is optimal ($C_{max} = r_6 + p_6 + q_6$).

Finally, the dependent jobs algorithm is based on the following proposition.

Proposition II.3

Let S be one Schrage schedule, and let $IC = [J_1, .., J_p]$ be a real critical path. If this path does not contain any dependent job, or if there are no jobs which verify the necessary conditions and Proposition II.2, then the theorem holds.

Proof:

If IC is a *real* critical path, then the makespan $C_{max} = r'_1 + \sum_{J_i \in IC} p_i + q_p$.

Let h_{IC} be $\min_{J_i \in IC} r'_i + \sum_{J_i \in IC} p_i + \min_{J_i \in IC} q_i$.

- If there is no critical job J_c such that $q_c < q_p$, then $q_p = \min_{J_i \in IC} q_i$. Therefore $C_{max} = h_{IC}$, since $r'_1 = \min_{J_i \in IC} r'_i$ (by construction of Schrage schedules, see [Carlier 82]). No job verifying the necessary conditions with a job in IC also verifies the conditions in Proposition II.2. Hence, the modified release dates of jobs on IC cannot be reduced without permanently increasing the makespan. Consequently, h_{IC} is a lower bound and the schedule is optimal.

- If J_c exists (c is the largest subscript such that $q_c < q_p$), let I be $[J_{c+1}, .., J_p]$. Then, $r'_i > t_c \; \forall J_i \in I$, otherwise J_c would have been set after at least one job of I in the modified Schrage algorithm (because $q_c < q_i, \; \forall J_i \in I$, since c is the largest subscript verifying $q_c < q_p$). As in the previous case, if conditions in Proposition II.3 are verified, no modified release date can be reduced such that relation $r'_i > t_c \; \forall J_i \in I$, is no longer verified. Therefore, in every schedule where J_c is placed in I, the makespan C'_{max} is greater than C_{max} :
$$C'_{max} \geq \min_{J_i \in I} r'_i + \sum_{J_i \in I} p_i + p_c + q_p > t_c + p_c + \sum_{J_i \in i} p_i + q_p = C_{max}.$$
Hence, in an optimal schedule, J_c has to be processed before or after all jobs of I. ♣

Actually, for each job J_i verifying the conditions in Proposition II.3, one can set $r_i = r'_i$, and Proposition II.3 becomes the theorem.

In our branch and bound algorithm, we are going to create every possible way of decreasing the start times of jobs on a *real* critical path IC, before applying the theorem to it. It is necessary to consider all the *artificial* critical paths before IC, and to use Proposition II.2.

Dependent jobs algorithm:

> *To each node v of the tree is associated a one-machine problem with a lower bound f_v (f is the value of the current lower bound).*
> *The upper bound f^{sup} is the value of the best solution known so far.*
> *$V =$Set of nodes.*
> **Initialization:**

> > $V := \phi$ *and* $v := 0$.
> > *Apply the modified Schrage algorithm to the problem (new release dates r') and compute the makespan C_{max}.*
> > **For all J_i which satisfy the necessary conditions, create an artificial critical path.**
> > *If it exists, search for the* **first** *critical path in which J_c exists.*
> > $I = [J_{c+1}, .., J_p]$.

> > > - *If J_p is the end of an* artificial *critical path, search for J_c such that $q_c + p_c < C_{max} - r_p - p_p$.*
> > > - *If J_p is the end of a* real *critical path, search for J_c such that $q_c < q_p$.*

> > $f_0 = h_I. \; f = f_0. \; f^{sup} = C_{max}.$

While J_c exists,

1. *If J_p is the end of an* artificial *critical path, consider two new problems, one in which J_c is required to be processed before J_p by setting:*

$$\mathbf{p_{cp}} := \mathbf{p_c}; \qquad (1)$$

and another one in which J_c is required to be processed after all jobs of I by setting:

$$\mathbf{p_{kc}} := \mathbf{p_k}, \ \forall \mathbf{J_k} \in \mathbf{I}. \quad (2)$$

If J_p is the end of a real *critical path, consider two new problems, one in which J_c is required to be processed before all jobs of I by setting:*

$$q_c := \max(q_c, \sum_{J_r \in I} p_r + q_p); \qquad (3)$$

and another in which J_c has to be processed after all jobs of I by setting:

$$r_c := \max(r_c, \min_{J_r \in I} r'_r + \sum_{J_r \in I} p_r). \qquad (4)$$

For each problem, compute the lower bound $f_\beta = \max(f, h_{I \bigcup \{J_c\}})$ and add a new node β (with the values r and not r') to V if $f_\beta < f^{sup}$.

Updating of r, q and minimal durations p before adding β.

2. $J_c = 0. \ f_v = 0.$
   While (J_c does not exist) and ($V \neq \phi$) and ($f^{sup} > f_v$), search in V for the node v with the lowest bound, remove v from V, apply the modified Schrage algorithm (r' values).
   If it exists, search for the **first** *critical path in which J_c exist. $I = [J_{c+1}, .., J_p]$ and $f = \max(f_v, h_I)$.*

   - *If J_p is the end of an* artificial *critical path, search for J_c such that $q_c + p_c < C_{max} - r_p - p_p$.*
   - *If J_p is the end of a* real *critical path, search for J_c such that $q_c < q_p$.*

$h_{I \bigcup \{J_c\}}$ is computed with the modified r_c. After each run of Schrage's algorithm, the computed makespan is stored if less than f^{sup}. The *first* critical path (*artificial or real*) is the one whose last job is, in the sequence given by the modified Schrage algorithm, before all the last jobs of other critical paths.

Expressions (1) and (2) are used both to put J_c before J_p or after I, and expressions (3) and (4) set J_c before or after I. All four **prevent any cycle from occurring in the algorithm.**

At the end of Step 1, updating is necessary since minimal durations have been changed in (1) or (2):

1. $p_{ij} := p_{ik} + p_{kj}$, whenever $p_{ij} < p_{ik} + p_{kj}$.
2. $r_j := r_i + p_{ij}$, whenever $p_{ij} > 0$ and $r_j < r_i + p_{ij}$.
3. $q_i := q_j + p_j + p_{ij} - p_i$, whenever $p_{ij} > 0$ and $q_i < q_j + p_j + p_{ij} - p_i$.

To improve the efficiency of the procedure, minimal durations are also modified when J_p is the end of a real critical path. Expression (2) is appended to expression (4), and

$$\mathbf{p_{ck}} := \mathbf{p_c}, \ \forall \mathbf{J_k} \in \mathbf{I} \quad (5)$$

is appended to expression (3).

We tested this procedure on job-shop problems solved with the Shifting Bottleneck procedure, and each time a One Machine problem had to be solved, we applied both Carlier's algorithm (CAR) and our algorithm (DEP), and compared the corresponding results.

Problem	Number of Operations	Number of Dependencies	CAR		DEP		Lower bound
			Value	Microruns	Value	Microruns	
1	10	6	1524	1	1473	3	1473
2	10	10	1540	2	1523	12	1523
3	10	22	1543	1	1529	14	1509
4	10	21	1511	1	1490	6	1476
5	20	75	1553	1	1531	1	1531
6	20	71	1372	4	1347	153	1347
7	20	83	1514	3	1402	43	1402
8	20	74	1434	1	1384	13	1384
9	20	70	1409	2	1372	1	1372
10	20	68	1447	1	1406	27	1403
11	20	64	1407	1	1347	3	1347
12	20	67	1464	5	1420	67	1401
13	20	75	1470	7	1403	12	1403
14	50	438	2969	75	2834	481	2816
15	50	454	2823	29	2762	14	2745
16	50	412	2988	1	2868	337	2807
17	50	503	3148	1	2958	328	2907
18	100	1841	5437	1	5401	129	5401
19	100	1953	5674	1	5618	19	5618
20	100	1404	5629	1	5506	1	5506

Value: Makespan of the best schedule obtained.
Microruns: Number of Schrage's algorithms applied.

Table II.1: Comparison between CAR and DEP.

As described in the beginning of this section, the makespan given in CAR corresponds to the length of the longest path without taking the dependencies into account, and is actually a lower bound. To obtain the real makespan in Table II.1, we need to introduce the dependencies in the sequence.

In Table II.1, we only gave some problems where the solutions given by CAR and DEP are different. Even if it occurs rarely (128 cases out of 3117), the variation can be large (see problem 7). Besides, we did not consider the case in which the real makespan in CAR and the makespan in DEP are the same, but greater than the lower bound.

Like CAR, DEP is an exponential algorithm. However, in our sample, the computing time was always less than 1 second, and very few problems (7 out of 3117) needed more than 100 microruns. Moreover, in nearly 87% of cases, the number of microruns was lower than or equal to the one in CAR. This number can be lower in DEP because the optimal sequence is sometimes found faster than in CAR, since the release dates are updated in Schrage's algorithm.

II.4.3 A Modified Shifting Bottleneck Procedure

The Modified Shifting Bottleneck (**MSB**) procedure is very close to **SB**. First, we replace Carlier's algorithm by the dependent job algorithm to detect and sequence the bottleneck machine, and also in the re-optimization step. In the latter step, the maximum number of local re-optimization cycles is increased from three to six. Finally, We also cancelled the second part of the local re-optimization procedure, where α noncritical machines are temporarily removed, because no real improvement has been found in doing so (almost the contrary because it is time consuming).

Let M_0 be the set of machines already scheduled, with associated selection S_p ($p \in M_0$), and let C_{max} be the corresponding makespan. In Step 1 of MSB, when $O(k, M_0)$ ($k \in M \backslash M_0$) is solved optimally (criterion $v(k, M_0)$, selection S_k), we ensure that C'_{max}, the makespan computed with the selections of $M_0 \bigcup \{k\}$, is such that: $C'_{max} = \max(C_{max}, v(k, M_0))$ (in classical SB, C'_{max} could be larger than C_{max} and $v(k, M_0)$). Hence, the machine k_g, such that $v(k_g, M_0) = \max\{v(k, M_0); k \in M \backslash M_0\}$, is the *real* bottleneck machine. Moreover, in the re-optimization step, let C_{max} (respectively C'_{max}) be the makespan before (respectively after) solving optimally each problem $O(k, M_0 \backslash \{k\})$ ($k \in M_0$). Again, we ensure that $C'_{max} \leq C_{max}$ (which is not always verified in SB).

Therefore, in the local re-optimization step, the makespan is now *monotone decreasing*. Even if the results of this MSB procedure are not always better than the original one (see Section II.4.4), its behavior does not fluctuate so much with the examples and the number of local re-optimization cycles. In other words, the new procedure is more *robust*.

II.4.4   Computational Experiments

II.4.4.1   The 10×10 and 5×20 Classical Examples

The first example is the notorious 10 jobs-10 machines problem ([Fisher and Thompson 63]) that resisted all procedures for a long time. In [Carlier and Pinson 89], for the first time and after a 22000 node exploration, the optimal value has been shown to be 930. The rule proposed in [Lageweg *et al.* 77] exhibits a schedule of length 1082, and most of other priority rules do worse. [Adams *et al.* 88], obtain a schedule of length 1015 with the standard version of the SB procedure (SBI) presented in this chapter, and the optimal value 930 with the enumerative version of SB (called SBII), very costly in terms of computing times. With our implementation of the SB procedure, we found a makespan of 974, and, with our MSB procedure, we get a schedule of length 950.

Nearly the same improvement has been found on the also well-known 20 jobs-5 machines problem ([Fisher and Thompson 63]), since we obtain a makespan of 1216 with MSB, 1240 with our version of SB, whereas [Adams *et al.* 88] found 1290.

II.4.4.2   Computational Results

A PASCAL implementation of SB, with at most three (SB1) and four (SB2) local re-optimization cycles in the local re-optimization step, and of the MSB procedure have been run on a SUN 4 workstation. These three procedures have been tested on problems either taken from the literature or randomly generated for this experiment (Table II.2).

Problems 1, 2 and 3 are from [Fisher and Thompson 63]. Problems 4-14 have the same routing for each job as in Problem 2 and processing times are randomly drawn from a uniform probability distribution on the interval [50,100] for Problems 4-12, and [25,100] for Problems 13 and 14. The routing for each job is randomly generated for all the other problems, with processing times randomly drawn from a uniform probability distribution on the interval [25,100] for Problem 15, on the interval [50,100] for Problem 16, on the interval [5,100] for Problem 17 and 18, on the interval [50,200] for Problem 19, and on the interval [5,100] for Problem 20.

First of all, note that most of the results are different (better or worse) in SB1 and SB2 (in 15 out the 20 cases). This confirms the *sensitivity* to the number of local re-optimization cycles. In contrast, when this number is switched from 6 to 4 (respectively 6 to 10) in MSB, the makespan is the same in 13 (respectively 17) out of the 20 cases. And, when there is a difference, it is not as important as between SB1 and SB2. Moreover, most of the time, MSB is better than SB1 or SB2, and nearly always better than the worst result of the two procedures. Finally, the computing times in MSB are smaller.

Problem	Number of			SB1		SB2		MSB	
				Value	CPU Sec	Value	CPU Sec	Value	CPU Sec
	Machines	Jobs	Operations	Value	Sec	Value	Sec	Value	Sec
1	6	6	36	55*	1	55*	1	55*	1
2	10	10	100	974	39	997	36	950	15
3	5	20	100	1240	17	1240	17	1216	8
4	10	10	100	1523	45	1440	42	1490	15
5	10	10	100	1411	40	1451	41	1355	13
6	10	10	100	1520	35	1537	40	1526	14
7	10	10	100	1501	36	1558	41	1540	17
8	10	10	100	1400	38	1430	42	1411	16
9	10	10	100	1482	34	1433	42	1485	15
10	10	10	100	1407	36	1467	42	1431	13
11	10	10	100	1543	39	1538	45	1526	16
12	10	10	100	1534	35	1504	37	1434	13
13	10	10	100	1182	41	1220	40	1212	16
14	10	10	100	1337	38	1357	45	1264	14
15	10	10	100	1158	33	1148	39	1133	15
16	10	10	100	1302	34	1386	38	1348	11
17	5	20	100	1288*	13	1288*	13	1288*	17
18	5	20	100	1162	9	1162	9	1158*	12
19	5	20	100	2776	12	2776	19	2670*	24
20	10	20	200	1414	214	1354	237	1394	59

Value: makespan of the best schedule obtained.
: value known to be optimal.

Table II.2: Comparison between SB1, SB2, and MSB.

II.4.5   Conclusion

We have presented an **MSB** procedure which is a new version of the Shifting Bottleneck procedure due to Adams, Balas and Zawack. We have tried to overcome some of the drawbacks of the latter, by taking account of *dependencies* between jobs to be sequenced on a particular machine. We enlarged the notion of *precedence* constraints between jobs, by defining the concept of **minimal duration** between start times of dependent jobs. A *new algorithm* is also proposed to optimally solve the One-Machine Sequencing problem with these general precedence constraints.

Using this *dependent job algorithm*, we ensure a monotone decrease of the makespan in the re-optimization step, and reduce the sensitivity of the Shifting Bottleneck procedure to the number of local re-optimization cycles so that the procedure is more robust. In the sample we considered, good results are reported, particularly for the celebrated 10×10 and 5×20 problems.

II.5   A Priority Rule-Based Dispatching Heuristic

In the iterative procedure presented in the next chapter (Section III.4.2), an other possibility to solve the problem at the scheduling level is to use list scheduling algorithms (see Section II.2.3.1). They are often very simple and require very short computing times.

The main part of this section is taken from [Conway *et al.* 67].

We implemented the classical procedure to generate schedules, described for instance in [Conway *et al.* 67]. We use the same notation, and call $\{S_{so}\}$ the set of *schedulable operations*, *i.e.*, the set of the operations which can be chosen at a given time. $\{S_{so}\}$ is a subset of the set of operations whose predecessors have been scheduled. When some operation is chosen in $\{S_{so}\}$, this operation is removed and replaced by the next operation in the routing, if any.

There are two ways of partitioning $\{S_{so}\}$: job and machine partitions. We chose machine partition, the most commonly used. $\{S_{so}\}$ is partitioned into m (number of machines) subsets $\{S_{so}^k\}$ containing the operations schedulable on machine k, *i.e.*, waiting in front of machine k. Some of these subsets may be empty during the procedure if no job is waiting at a given time, or if all the operations of these machines have been processed.

Let $\{S_{ip}\}$ be the set of *in-process* operations, that can also be partitioned into m subset $\{S_{ip}^k\}$ with a single element (since a machine can only process one job at a time). C_k denotes he completion time of the operation in $\{S_{ip}^k\}$, r_{ijk} the release date (the completion time of the previous operation in the routing or 0 if it is the first operation) of operation o_{ijk} in $\{S_{so}^k\}$, and p_{ijk} the processing time of this operation.

Then, $\max(C_k, r_{ijk})$ and $\max(C_k, r_{ijk}) + p_{ijk}$ are the respective minimum start time and completion time of operation o_{ijk} in $\{S_{so}^k\}$.

There are two main methods to determine the subset $\{S_{so}^k\}$ in which the next operation will be selected:

1. $\{S_{so}^k\} \neq \phi$ is selected with the criterion

$$\min_k \min_{o_{ijk} \in \{S_{so}^k\}} [\max(C_k, r_{ijk})].$$

This procedure generates **nondelay** schedules.

2. $\{S_{so}^k\} \neq \phi$ is selected with the criterion

$$\min_k \min_{o_{ijk} \in \{S_{so}^k\}} [\max(C_k, r_{ijk}) + p_{ijk}].$$

This procedure generates **active** schedules.

The operation in $\{S_{so}^k\}$ is chosen according to a priority rule, based on the characteristics of the operation, or of the associated job. Actually, this type of procedure generates a schedule by simulating the job-shop.

Numerous rules have been proposed and studied in the literature. We consider only the following four, very simple rules:

1. **FIFO** (First In, First Out): select the operation arrived first in front of the machine, *i.e.*, select o_{ijk} in $\{S_{so}^k\}$ with the smallest r_{ijk}.

2. **SPT** (Shortest Processing Time): select the operation with the smallest processing time, *i.e.*, select o_{ijk} in $\{S_{so}^k\}$ with the smallest p_{ijk}.

3. **LPT** (Longest Processing Time): select the operation with the longest processing time, *i.e.*, select o_{ijk} in $\{S_{so}^k\}$ with the largest p_{ijk}.

4. **MWKR** (Most Work Remaining): select the operation corresponding to the job on which the largest amount of work remain to be done, *i.e.*, select o_{ijk} in $\{S_{so}^k\}$ with the largest delivery time q_{ijk}.

II.6   Conclusion

After having discussed various methods to solve the job-shop scheduling problem, two heuristics (*to* be used in later chapters) have been presented. The Modified Shifting Bottleneck (MSB) procedure shows good performance, but with computing times very sensitive to the size of the problem. In order to consider very large (practical) problems, we have also presented a Priority Rule-based Dispatching (PRD) heuristic with simple rules. In general, this heuristic will not find very good solutions but is easy to implement and requires small computing times.

With this difference in quality of the solutions obtained with the two heuristics, in chapter IV, we will be able to show the impact of the scheduling algorithm on the quality of the solution given by the iterative procedure described in the Section III.4.2.

*

*   *

Chapter III

An Integrated Planning and Scheduling Model

*There appear to be good opportunities for research on
the interface between scheduling and inventory theory.
Both ... have been developed in complete mutual isolation.*

Lenstra J.K., Rinnoy Kan A.H.G.

III.1 Introduction

Many manufacturing companies are heavily penalized by the amount of Work-in-Process (WIP) and delays in the workshops. No matter how sophisticated, a scheduling method, which by definition operates at the *operational level* in the hierarchy, will have a limited efficiency since these delays and large WIP are a consequence of higher level decisions, in particular the tactical planning level decisions.

As already quoted from [Hax and Candea 84] in Chapter I, among the requirements for a successfull MRP procedure .. *A feasible master production schedule must be drawn up, or else the accumulated planned orders of components might "bump" into the resource restrictions and become infeasible. [Smith 78] points out that the lack of appropriate support for managers to produce good master schedules is a major weakness of MRP, and probably the biggest source of disappointment in the performance of such systems."*

The issue is the **consistency** of decisions taken at different decision levels in the hierarchy. If this issue has been investigated in *Aggregate Planning* (see *e.g.*, [Bitran and Tirupati 93]) where the two (detailed and aggregate) decisions levels are of the same type, very few results concern the consistency of planning and scheduling decisions which are very different in nature. The methodology presented in the following chapters is an attempt to address this issue.

It is remarkable that in both the literature and practice, mid-term planning and scheduling issues are treated in sequence and **independently** of each other (see [Lenstra and Rinnooy Kan 84] or [Buxey 89]). There has been no systematic treatment of the consistency issue between those two decision levels. In most standard hierarchical approaches, one first determines a production *plan*, and then tries to find a *schedule* compatible with that plan, *i.e.*, such that the planned quantities are produced without delays. This kind of approach can be viewed as a **one-pass** procedure where the planning level model has a very aggregate view of the detailed model of the workshop. Indeed, in most planning models, the capacity constraints are simplistic or naive, for exact capacity constraints in terms of the aggregate variables (quantitites to produce) are not available. The exact capacity of the workshop also depends on the sequencing of operations on the machines. Thus, it may not be wise to determine an "optimal" solution at the planning level if this decision is not achievable at the lower (scheduling) level.

More recently, some work has been done to take into account the relationship between the planning and scheduling decision levels (see [Afentakis 85], [Gershwin 89], [Fontan and Imbert 85] and [Van Wassenhove and Potts 91]). However, there are few analytical models which ensure that there exists a schedule compatible with the production plan.

Integrating both levels is difficult since, in general, the planning models are **continuous** (one deals with **flows** of products, *i.e.*, *how much* to produce) whereas the scheduling models are **discrete** (one deals with the ordering of operations on the machines, *i.e.*, *when and how* to produce). Even for the simple one-machine ELSP (Economic Lot Scheduling Problem, see [Elmaghraby 78] or [Zipkin 91]), characterizing an optimal solution is still an open problem.

Moreover, if the horizon is long and the number of products is large, it may not be wise to define a detailed integrated model, since the data would not be reliable over the entire horizon. In this case, an integrated approach would make sense with an intermediate decision level between the traditional planning level and the scheduling level. However, the consistency issue is then postponed to these two planning levels.

Here, we define a *coherent* methodology for planning and scheduling where:

- as in previous approaches, one determines a production plan at a tactical level **but** one also ensures that this plan is achievable, *i.e.*, there exists at least one **feasible** schedule, *i.e.*, compatible with that plan.

- one determines a schedule at the operational level. By construction of the production plan, one knows that there exists at least one feasible schedule.

In contrast to previous approaches, **one guarantees that the production plan is achievable,** *i.e.*, there exists at least one feasible schedule. On the other hand, it may happen that all the demands are not satisfied, in particular if the capacity of the workshop is not sufficiently large.

It is worth noting that the scheduling decision level is not suppressed. To provide a feasible production plan, this integrated model incorporates scheduling decisions over an horizon usually longer than the standard scheduling horizon at the operational level. Once computed, this production plan (or some part of this production plan over a shorter horizon) is still an input to the operational level. The difference is that this plan is feasible.

We present a new method to treat *simultaneously* planning and scheduling decisions in a job-shop environment. The basic idea is to observe that, for a **fixed** sequence of operations on the machines, the capacity constraints of the workshop are **easily** expressed in terms of the planning variables (quantities to produce at each period). They are just linear constraints in terms of these variables. This property is then used in an iterative procedure which alternates between

- solving a **planning problem** where the exact capacity constraints are stated for a **fixed** sequence y of operations on the machines (selection $S(y)$). This problem is a standard Linear Programming problem, easy to solve even for large problems. The production plan, optimal solution to this problem, is **achievable** by definition. Indeed, there exists at least one feasible schedule (using the sequence y) to achieve that plan. Of course, other feasible schedules may also exist.

- solving a standard **scheduling problem** for a **fixed** production plan. Here, one tries to find a sequence y' better than y (what "better" means will become clear later). This problem being $\mathcal{NP}$-hard, for efficiency reasons, a heuristic is used at this level.

We first present the notation used in the models at both planning and scheduling levels. Then, the integrated planning and scheduling model is translated into a linear model in continuous variables when there is no set-up time and in mixed-integer variables otherwise. Some of the constraints state the *necessary and sufficient conditions* for the production plan to be achievable, *i.e.*, they state that there exists a feasible schedule to achieve that plan. To simplify the resolution, we derive simpler *necessary* conditions as well as *sufficient* conditions. The latter conditions will then be used in the iterative procedure mentionned earlier. We also show that this iterative procedure converges to a local optimum if the sequence of problems at both levels are solved optimally (*ideal* procedure). Finally, first experimental results are presented.

III.2   Notation and Definitions

III.2.1   Job-Shop Scheduling

As already discussed in the previous chapter, job-shop scheduling means *sequencing* a set of *jobs* J on a set of *machines* M. Each job J_j corresponds to a *lot* of items j to be processed. One wishes to minimize the total amount of time C_{max} (or *makespan*) required to process all the jobs. The routing of operations on the machines is fixed and, on each machine, only one job can be processed at a time.

For the problem under consideration, we first recall and adapt the notation already used in Chapter II:

$J = \{J_1, J_2, .., J_n\}$ is the set of n jobs to be processed.

$M = \{1, 2, .., m\}$ is the set of machines.

o_{ijk} is the jth operation of job J_i to be processed on machine $k \in M$.

N is the set of operations (with 0 and * as *"start"* and *"finish"* operations).

A is the set of pairs of operations subject to precedence constraints in the routing.

E_k is the set of pairs of operations to be processed on machine k.

p_{ijk}^u is the per unit (of product i) processing time of operation o_{ijk} and p_{ijk}^t is the *total* duration. τ_{ijk} is the set-up time on machine k of operation o_{ijk}.

t_{ijk} is the starting time of operation o_{ijk}.

The problem can be formulated as follows:

$$O \begin{cases} \min t_* \\ t_{ijk} - t_{ij'k'} \geq p_{ij'k'}^t & \forall(o_{ij'k'}, o_{ijk}) \in A \\ t_{ijk} \geq 0 & \forall o_{ijk} \in N \\ t_{ijk} - t_{i'j'k} \geq p_{i'j'k}^t \ or \ t_{i'j'k} - t_{ijk} \geq p_{ijk}^t & \forall(o_{i'j'k}, o_{ijk}) \in E_k, \ k \in M \end{cases}$$

Any feasible solution of (O) is a **schedule**.

As already mentionned in Chapter II, this problem can be represented with a disjunctive graph (see [Roy and Sussman 64]) $G = (N, A, E)$, with N as the set of nodes, A the set of conjunctive arcs and E the set of disjunctive arcs (see the exemple in Figure III-1 with 4 machines and 5 jobs).

Recall that:

- A **selection** S_k in E_k contains exactly one member of each pair of disjunctive arcs of E_k.

- A **complete selection** S corresponds to a union of selections S_k, one in each E_k, $k \in M$.

- every sequence is associated to an acyclic complete selection S.

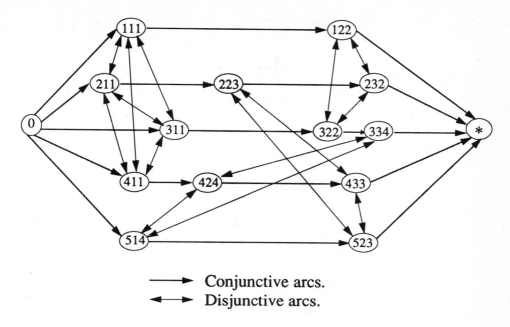

   ⟶ Conjunctive arcs.
   ⟷ Disjunctive arcs.

Figure III-1: Disjunctive graph.

III.2.2 Planning

We consider a planning problem with n products on a discretized finite planning horizon of T periods. Each period t is an interval of c_t time units, in which production can take place.

The demand D_{it} for each product i and at each period t is assumed to be given. Let X_{it} be the amount of product i to be processed before the end of period t, and let I_{it} be the inventory level of product i at the end of period t.

The problem is represented in Figure III-2, where $H = \sum_{t=1}^{T} c_t$, with $X_t = [X_{it} : i = 1, .., n]$, $I_t = [I_{it} : i = 1, .., n]$, and $D_t = [D_{it} : i = 1, .., n]$.

One wishes to minimize an objective (or cost) function $g(X, I)$, whose arguments $X = [X_t : t = 1, .., T]$ and $I = [I_t : t = 1, .., T]$ are the vectors of amounts of production and inventory levels respectively.

A standard linear form of g is:

$$\sum_{i,t} c_{it}^+ . I_{it}^+ + c_{it}^- . I_{it}^- + c_{it}^{pr} . X_{it}$$

where $I_{it} = I_{it}^+ - I_{it}^-$ ($I_{it}^+, I_{it}^- \geq 0$). I_{it}^+ stands for the *physical* inventory *on hand* of product i at the end of period t. On the other hand, I_{it}^- is the *backlog* or *shortage* of

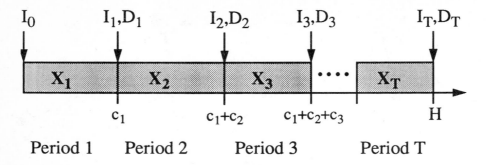

Figure III-2: Planning problem.

product i at the end of period t, and therefore corresponds to unsatisfied demands that will eventually be satisfied later (with some delay).

Equivalently: $I_{it}^+ = \max(0, I_{it})$ and $I_{it}^- = |\min(0, I_{it})|$.

c_{it}^+ is a per unit holding cost for product i at period t.
c_{it}^- is a per unit backlogging cost for product i at period t
c_{it}^{pr} is a per unit production cost for product i at period t.

Of course, this objective function g could be more complicated, and for example, could include costs associated with set-up times.

If we ignore the capacity constraints from the operational level, *i.e.*, those which guarantee the existence of a feasible schedule, the planning problem is:

$$
\begin{cases}
\min \displaystyle\sum_{t=1}^{T} \sum_{i=1}^{n} (c_{it}^+ . I_{it}^+ + c_{it}^- . I_{it}^- + c_{it}^{pr} . X_{it}) & & \\
(I_{it}^+ - I_{it}^-) - (I_{it-1}^+ - I_{it-1}^-) - X_{it} + D_{it} = 0 & i = 1,..,n; t = 1,..,T & (1) \\
X_{it} \geq 0 & \forall i, t & (2) \\
I_{it}^+ \geq 0 & \forall i, t & (3) \\
I_{it}^- \geq 0 & \forall i, t & (4)
\end{cases}
$$

where I_0 is the initial inventory level vector.

(1) is the standard inventory balance equation.

A number of other constraints can be incorporated to take into account eventual extra capacity available with overtime hours or subcontracting for example.

A solution to this problem is a production plan P=(X,I) that determines the amounts of production at each period as well as the inventory levels at the end of each period.

In general, in the literature on planning models, the capacity constraints are aggregate. For example, in a classical model described in [Bitran and Tirupati 93], the capacity constraints include regular and overtime hours, and the planning problem is then

$$
\begin{cases}
\min \sum_{t=1}^{T} \sum_{i=1}^{n} (c_{it}^+ . I_{it}^+ + c_{it}^- . I_{it}^- + c_{it}^{pr} . X_{it}) + \sum_{t=1}^{T} (r_t . R_t + o_t . O_t) & \\
(I_{it}^+ - I_{it}^-) - (I_{it-1}^+ - I_{it-1}^-) - X_{it} + D_{it} & = 0 & i = 1, .., n; t = 1, .., T & (1) \\
X_{it} & \geq 0 & \forall i, t & (2) \\
I_{it}^+ & \geq 0 & \forall i, t & (3) \\
I_{it}^- & \geq 0 & \forall i, t & (4) \\
\sum_{i=1}^{n} (m_i . X_{it}) & \leq R_t + O_t & t = 1, .., T & (5) \\
R_t & \leq rm_t & t = 1, .., T & (6) \\
O_t & \leq om_t & t = 1, .., T & (7) \\
R_t & \geq 0 & \forall t & (8) \\
O_t & \geq 0 & \forall t & (9)
\end{cases}
$$

where

R_t (respectively O_t) is the number of *regular* (repectively *overtime*) hours used in period t.

r_t (respectively o_t) is the per unit cost of *regular* (respectively *overtime*) production in period t.

rm_t (respectively om_t) is the maximum number of available *regular* (repectively *overtime*) hours in period t.

m_i is the number of hours needed to process one unit of product i.

Obviously, nothing in this model guarantees that a feasible production plan (including the optimal one) is achievable, *i.e.*, that there exists a feasible schedule compatible with that plan. The reason is that the only information about the workshop is contained in the processing times on the machines and the available working hours. In particular, nothing is said about the routing of the products and the conflicts on the machines, a crucial information for feasibility of a production plan.

In the integrated model to be presented below, we model the exact capacity constraints through a detailed representation of the workshop. Then, an iterative procedure is described to solve the problem.

III.3 Integrating Planning and Scheduling Decisions

III.3.1 Introduction

In this section we present several ways of integrating in the planning model detailed capacity constraints induced by the workshop topology and the sequencing decisions.

We first consider *necessary and sufficient* conditions of feasibility of a production plan that theoretically permit to obtain a **global** optimal solution to the problem $min_{y \in Y} \ g(X, I)$ (where Y is the set of all possible sequences of products on the machines). On a practical point of of view, those conditions are useless since the associated problem becomes untractable.

Necessary, conditions are also stated, but they do not restrict sufficiently the set of feasible production plans. A production plan, solution to this simplified problem, is not guaranteed to be achievable either.

Finally, also simpler *sufficient* conditions can be written by **fixing** in advance a particular sequence of products on the machines. Indeed, in doing so, exact detailed capacity constraints are easily expressed in terms of the X vector. Based on these conditions, an iterative procedure is derived in Section III.4.2.

Let us first derive the feasibility conditions on the production plan induced by the detailed capacity constraints at the operational (scheduling) level.

III.3.2   Multi-Period Scheduling

The workshop defined in Section III.2.1, is replicated on the T periods of the discretized planning horizon. We then modify the notation as follows:

$J^t = \{J_{1t}, .., J_{nt}\}$ is the set of n jobs to be completed *in period t*.
o_{ijkt} is the jth operation of job J_{it} to be processed on machine $k \in M$.
p^u_{ijkt} is the *per unit of product* processing time of operation o_{ijkt}, and p^t_{ijkt} is the *total* processing time.
τ_{ijkt} is the set-up time on the machine where operation o_{ijkt} is processed.
t_{ijkt} is the starting time of operation o_{ijkt}.
L is the set of last operations in the routing of the jobs.

The graph in Figure III-3 displays the problem in Figure III-1 replicated on three periods. For the sake of simplicity, we have not displayed, on this graph, the disjunctive arcs linking all the operations to be processed on a same machine and belonging to jobs of different periods (for example, operations o_{1111} and o_{1112}).

In the case where the set-up times are null or neglected, the production plan P=(X,I) is translated as input data for the scheduling problem via the relation

$$p^t_{ijkt} = p^u_{ijkt}.X_{it}$$

This relation states that the *total* processing time of an operation is the *per unit of product* processing time, **times** the amount of products in this operation.

Moreover, only c_t units of time are available in each period t. Thus, the jobs of the first period must be completed by c_1, those of period 2 must be completed by $c_1 + c_2$, and so on ... (see Figure III-4).

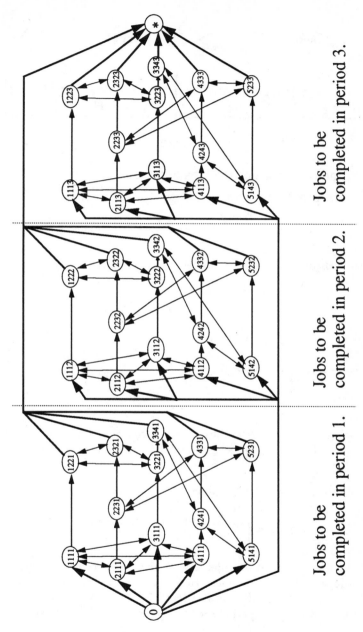

Figure III-3: Multi-period scheduling.

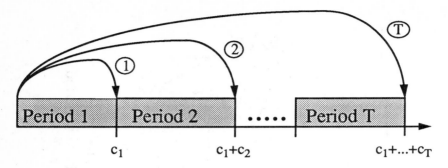

t : Interval in which the jobs of period t can
       be processed.

Figure III-4: Representation of due dates.

Thus, the scheduling problem can be stated in terms of the production plan variables as follows:

$$
O_1 \begin{cases}
t_{ijkt} - t_{ij'k't} - p^u_{ij'k't}.X_{it} & \geq 0 \quad \forall(o_{ij'k't}, o_{ijkt}) \in A \quad (1) \\
t_{ijkt} & \geq 0 \quad \forall o_{ijkt} \in N \quad (2) \\
\begin{cases}
t_{ijkt} - t_{i'j'kt'} - p^u_{i'j'kt'}.X_{i't'} \geq 0 \\
or \\
t_{i'j'kt'} - t_{ijkt} - p^u_{ijkt}.X_{it} \geq 0
\end{cases} & \forall(o_{i'j'kt'}, o_{ijkt}) \in E_k, \ k \in M \quad (3) \\
t_{ijkt} + p^u_{ijkt}.X_{it} & \leq \sum_{l=1}^{t} c_l \quad \forall o_{ijkt} \in L \quad (4)
\end{cases}
$$

Conditions (4) state that the jobs must be completed by the end of their respective period. They summarize the detailed *exact* capacity constraints on the production plan X.

If the set-up times are not negligible, (O_1) must be reformulated using:

$$
p^t_{ijkt} = \begin{cases}
p^u_{ijkt}.X_{it} + \tau_{ijkt} & if \ X_{it} > 0 \\
0 & if \ X_{it} = 0
\end{cases}
$$

Several hypotheses can be considered to define the precedence relations between operations of jobs of different periods. Here, we consider that a job which must be *completed* by the end of period t can be *started* in previous periods.

In Chapter IV, two multi-period scheduling policies are considered:

- the problem is solved globally without any particular precedence constraint between operations of different periods.

- in the second policy, an operation o_{ijkt} can be started only if all the operations on the same machine k and from previous periods $(< t)$ have been completed.

From now on and until Section III.3.6, we assume that set-up times are negligible.

III.3.3 A Linear Model in Continuous Variables

In the integrated planning and scheduling model of a job-shop, we must integrate the constraints described in (O_1) in the planning model so that the problem to solve is now:

$$
P_{NSC} \begin{cases}
\min \sum_{t=1}^{T} \sum_{i=1}^{n} (c_{it}^{+}.I_{it}^{+} + c_{it}^{-}.I_{it}^{-} + c_{it}^{pr}.X_{it}) & \\
(I_{it}^{+} - I_{it}^{-}) - (I_{it-1}^{+} - I_{it-1}^{-}) - X_{it} + D_{it} = 0 & i = 1,..,n; t = 1,..,T & (1) \\
X_{it} \geq 0 & \forall i, t & (2) \\
I_{it}^{+} \geq 0 & \forall i, t & (3) \\
I_{it}^{-} \geq 0 & \forall i, t & (4) \\
t_{ijkt} - t_{ij'k't} - p_{ij'k't}^{u}.X_{it} \geq 0 & \forall(o_{ij'k't}, o_{ijkt}) \in A & (5) \\
t_{ijkt} \geq 0 & \forall o_{ijkt} \in N & (6) \\
\begin{cases} t_{ijkt} - t_{i'j'kt'} - p_{i'j'kt'}^{u}.X_{i't'} \geq 0 \\ or \\ t_{i'j'kt'} - t_{ijkt} - p_{ijkt}^{u}.X_{it} \geq 0 \end{cases} & \forall(o_{i'j'kt'}, o_{ijkt}) \in E_k, \ k \in M & (7) \\
t_{ijkt} + p_{ijkt}^{u}.X_{it} \leq \sum_{l=1}^{t} c_l & \forall o_{ijkt} \in L & (9)
\end{cases}
$$

As already explained in Section II.2.2, each disjunctive constraint can be modeled using two conjunctive constraints and an associated Boolean variable.

In doing so (7) becomes:

$$
\begin{cases}
t_{ijkt} - t_{i'j'kt'} - p_{i'j'kt'}^{u}.X_{i't'} \geq -B.y_{ijkt,i'j'kt'} & (7) \\
t_{i'j'kt'} - t_{ijkt} - p_{ijkt}^{u}.X_{it} \geq -B.(1 - y_{ijkt,i'j'kt'}) & (8)
\end{cases} \quad \forall(o_{i'j'kt'}, o_{ijkt}) \in E_k, \ k \in M
$$

The constraints (9) ensure that the production X_{it} of a job J_{it} is completed by the end of period t. However, such a job cannot be completed before the beginning of period t otherwise the inventory balance equation is meaningless. If it was the case, the production X_{it} should be part of a job of a previous period.

Therefore, in (P_{NSC}) we must impose the additional constraint:

$$
t_{ijkt} + p_{ijkt}^{u}.X_{it} \geq \sum_{l=1}^{t-1} c_l \quad \forall o_{ijkt} \in L \quad (10)
$$

These constraints state that the last operations of jobs J_{it} must be completed in period t and <u>not</u> before.

Solving a *simple* scheduling problem with mixed-integer variables is already difficult, so that solving (P_{NSC}) with a standard mixed-integer LP package is not possible for realistic size problems. Therefore, another approach is required and is developed in the sequel.

III.3.4   Necessary Conditions

To simplify the resolution, necessary conditions can be used instead of the necessary and sufficient conditions that involve disjunctive constraints.

The solution of this simplified problem, *i.e.*, a production plan $P^* = (X^*, I^*)$, is searched for in a set (Ω_{NC}) of admissible plans larger than the set (Ω_{NSC}) generated by the necessary and sufficient conditions. More precisely, $\Omega_{NSC} \subset \Omega_{NC}$. But the feasibility of P^* is not guaranteed any more.

The formulation using only necessary conditions is now:

$$
P_{NC} \begin{cases}
\min \sum_{t=1}^{T} \sum_{i=1}^{n} (c_{it}^+ . I_{it}^+ + c_{it}^- . I_{it}^- + c_{it}^{pr} . X_{it}) & \\
(I_{it}^+ - I_{it}^-) - (I_{it-1}^+ - I_{it-1}^-) - X_{it} + D_{it} & = 0 & i = 1,..,n; t = 1,..,T & (1) \\
X_{it} & \geq 0 & \forall i,t & (2) \\
I_{it}^+ & \geq 0 & \forall i,t & (3) \\
I_{it}^- & \geq 0 & \forall i,t & (4) \\
t_{ijkt} - t_{ij'k't} - p_{ij'k't}^u . X_{it} & \geq 0 & \forall (o_{ij'k't}, o_{ijkt}) \in A & (5) \\
t_{ijkt} & \geq 0 & \forall o_{ijkt} \in N & (6) \\
\sum_{l=1}^{t} (\sum_{o_{ijkl} \in O_{kl}} p_{ijkl}^u . X_{il}) & \leq \sum_{l=1}^{t} c_l & \forall k \in M, \forall t & (7) \\
t_{ijkt} + p_{ijkt}^u . X_{it} & \leq \sum_{l=1}^{t} c_l & \forall o_{ijkt} \in L & (9) \\
t_{ijkt} + p_{ijkt}^u . X_{it} & \geq \sum_{l=1}^{t-1} c_l & \forall o_{ijkt} \in L & (10)
\end{cases}
$$

where O_{kl} is the set of operations of period l to be processed on machine k.

We keep the conditions (5) which corresponds to the conjunctive constraints induced by the routing of products on the machines.

Conditions (7) that the sum of processing times of operations to be processed on the same machine cannot be larger than the time available. Let us illustrate below those conditions on an example.

Example III.1
Consider the example in Figure III-1, replicated on three periods in Figure III-3. For instance, on machine 1, the sum of processing times of operations of period 1

must be less than c_1.

$$p_{1111} + p_{2111} + p_{3111} + p_{4111} \leq c_1$$

Similarly, for the operations of the first two periods we must have:

$$p_{1111} + p_{2111} + p_{3111} + p_{4111} + p_{1112} + p_{2112} + p_{3112} + p_{4112} \leq c_1 + c_2$$

These conditions should improve the quality of the production plan which usually is computed in ignoring the detail of the workshop. Here, at least some information about the workshop is used. However, it is unlikely that an optimal solution to (P_{NC}) is feasible and we are primarily interested in such a solution.

III.3.5 Sufficient Conditions

Another way to simplify the resolution of (P_{NSC}) is to consider *simpler* sufficient conditions. In this case, the set Ω_{SC} of admissible plans is a subset of Ω_{NSC} generated when using the necessary and sufficient conditions ($\Omega_{SC} \subset \Omega_{NSC}$).

Using such conditions, if on the one hand, an optimal solution P^* is unlikely to be optimal for (P_{NSC}), on the other hand, P^* is **feasible** and hopefully easier to compute.

A set of sufficient conditions is generated by *imposing* a fixed sequence of operations on the machines when a choice has to be made. In other words, before computing the production plan, we resolve the possible conflicts of operations on the machines. We choose a particular sequence $y \in Y$, *i.e.*, an acyclic complete selection $S(y)$. In doing so, all the disjunctive arcs of E are replaced by conjunctive arcs. Therefore, the computational complexity induced by the choice of a direction for each disjunctive arc in (P_{NSC}) is eliminated.

The problem is now formulated as follows:

$$P_{SC}(y) \begin{cases} \min \sum_{t=1}^{T} \sum_{i=1}^{n} (c_{it}^+ . I_{it}^+ + c_{it}^- . I_{it}^- + c_{it}^{pr} . X_{it}) \\ (I_{it}^+ - I_{it}^-) - (I_{it-1}^+ - I_{it-1}^-) - X_{it} + D_{it} = 0 \quad i = 1,..,n; t = 1,..,T \quad (1) \\ X_{it} \geq 0 \quad \forall i,t \quad (2) \\ I_{it}^+ \geq 0 \quad \forall i,t \quad (3) \\ I_{it}^- \geq 0 \quad \forall i,t \quad (4) \\ t_{ijkt} - t_{ij'k't} - p_{ij'k't}^u . X_{it} \geq 0 \quad \forall (o_{ij'k't}, o_{ijkt}) \in A \quad (5) \\ t_{ijkt} \geq 0 \quad \forall o_{ijkt} \in N \quad (6) \\ t_{ijkt} - t_{i'j'kt'} - p_{i'j'kt'}^u . X_{i't'} \geq 0 \quad \forall (o_{i'j'kt'}, o_{ijkt}) \in S(y) \quad (7) \\ t_{ijkt} + p_{ijkt}^u . X_{it} \leq \sum_{l=1}^{t} c_l \quad \forall o_{ijkt} \in L \quad (9) \\ t_{ijkt} + p_{ijkt}^u . X_{it} \geq \sum_{l=1}^{t-1} c_l \quad \forall o_{ijkt} \in L \quad (10) \end{cases}$$

A plan P^*, solution to $P_{SC}(y)$, is feasible by construction. Indeed, there exists at least one schedule (using the sequence y) that achieves that plan.

Remark III.1

It is worth noting that $P_{SC}(y)$ is always well-defined ($X = 0$ is always an admissible solution) except for the sequences y in which the last operation $o_{ijkt} \in L$ of some job J_{it}, precedes some operation of some other job $J_{jt'}$ with $t' < t - 1$. Therefore, an admissible sequence y must be such that all the last operations of jobs $J_{it} \in J^t$ cannot be processed before any operation of any job $J_{jt'}$ with $t' < t - 1$.

Proof: Assume that, in a sequence y, an operation $o_{ijkt} \in L$ has been sequenced before an operation $o_{i'j'kt'}$, and $t' < t - 1$.

$$(7) \Rightarrow t_{i'j'kt'} \geq t_{ijkt} + p^u_{ijkt}.X_{it}$$

and

$$(10) \Rightarrow t_{ijkt} \geq \sum_{l=1}^{t-1} c_l - p^u_{ijkt}.X_{it}$$

so that,

$$t_{i'j'kt'} \geq \sum_{l=1}^{t-1} c_l - p^u_{ijkt}.X_{it} + p^u_{ijkt}.X_{it} = \sum_{l=1}^{t-1} c_l$$

a contradiction with (9) applied to $t_{i'j'kt'}$

$$t_{i'j'kt'} \leq \sum_{l=1}^{t'} c_l$$

since $t' < t - 1$. ♣

Remark III.2

As a matter of fact, the set $\Omega_{SC}(y)$ of admissibles plans for $P_{SC}(y)$ is the set of plans in Ω_{NSC} that are feasible for $S(y)$. Therefore, the quality of a solution P^* to $P_{SC}(y)$ strongly depends on the choice of the sequence y.

Depending on the chosen sequence y, P^* might be a very poor production plan and therefore, a one-pass method solving $P_{SC}(y)$ for a single sequence y is not likely to yield good results. An iterative method is described in the sequel.

III.3.6   An Integrated Model with Set-Up Times

We do not assume that the set-up times are negligible any more. Taking into account the set-up times requires the introduction of Boolean variables, thus transforming P_{NSC}, P_{NC} and P_{SC} into mixed-integer linear programs. We only describe the new formulation of P_{SC}.

Let y_{it} be the Boolean variable which takes the value 1 if $X_{it} > 0$ and 0 otherwise. In case of set-up time, let Δ_{it} be the cost associated with this set-up time penalization.

$P_{SC}(y)$ is then modified as follows:

$$
P^{tp}_{SC}(y) \begin{cases}
\min \sum\limits_{t=1}^{T} \sum\limits_{i=1}^{n} (c_{it}^{+}.I_{it}^{+} + c_{it}^{-}.I_{it}^{-} + c_{it}^{pr}.X_{it} + y_{it}.\Delta_{it}) \\
(I_{it}^{+} - I_{it}^{-}) - (I_{it-1}^{+} - I_{it-1}^{-}) - X_{it} + D_{it} & = 0 & i = 1,..,n; t = 1,..,T & (1) \\
X_{it} & \geq 0 & \forall i,t & (2) \\
I_{it}^{+} & \geq 0 & \forall i,t & (3) \\
I_{it}^{-} & \geq 0 & \forall i,t & (4) \\
t_{ijkt} - t_{ij'k't} - p_{ij'k't}^{u}.X_{it} - \tau_{ij'k't}.y_{it} & \geq 0 & \forall (o_{ij'k't}, o_{ijkt}) \in A & (5) \\
t_{ijkt} & \geq 0 & \forall o_{ijkt} \in N & (6) \\
t_{ijkt} - t_{i'j'kt'} - p_{i'j'kt'}^{u}.X_{it'} - \tau_{i'j'kt'}.y_{i't'} & \geq 0 & \forall (o_{i'j'kt'}, o_{ijkt}) \in S(y) & (7) \\
t_{ijkt} + p_{ijkt}^{u}.X_{it} + \tau_{ijkt}.y_{it} & \leq \sum\limits_{l=1}^{t} c_l & \forall o_{ijkt} \in L & (9) \\
t_{ijkt} + p_{ijkt}^{u}.X_{it} + \tau_{ijkt}.y_{it} & \geq \sum\limits_{l=1}^{t-1} c_l & \forall o_{ijkt} \in L & (10) \\
(\sum\limits_{l=t}^{T} D_{il}).y_{it} - X_{it} & \geq 0 & i = 1,..,n; t = 1,..,T & (11) \\
y_{it} & \in \{0,1\} & \forall i,t & (12)
\end{cases}
$$

Constraints (11) ensure that $y_{it} = 1$ if $X_{it} > 0$.

Remarks III.1 and III.2 are still valid with this formulation.

III.4   Solving Procedures

III.4.1   A One-Pass Procedure

We know that, in solving $P_{SC}(y)$ for the fixed sequence y, the resulting plan $P = (X, I)$ will be optimal with respect to this sequence. This plan is **feasible** for there exists at least one schedule (using the sequence y) which is compatible with that plan, *i.e.*, all the jobs J_i associated with P are completed by their due date. However, some demands may not be satisfied. As already discussed in Section III.2, the quality of the result strongly depends on the chosen sequence y.

Therefore, a simple **one-pass** procedure can be deduced. A possible choice of the sequence y is as follows:

1. Solve $P_{SC}(y)$ with only constraints (1-4), *i.e.* ignoring the scheduling problem. The resulting plan P^* is an *ideal plan* since no capacity contraint from the operational level is taken into account.

2. Given this plan P^*, find a sequence y^* which minimizes the makespan (*i.e.*, solve (O_1)). In general, P^* is not feasible and some jobs will be completed after their due date.

3. Solve $P_{SC}(y^*)$, and take any optimal solution P_1 as final production plan. This plan is now *feasible* since the constraints (9) are satisfied for the sequence y^*.

As the sequence y^* is optimal (for the makespan criterion) for the *ideal plan* P^*, one may conjecture that y^* is a good choice. The unfeasible *ideal plan* P^* is *adapted* to the capacity constraints (9) (for the sequence y^*) to yield a fesible plan P_1.

The first part of the procedure could still be refined in computing an *ideal plan* P^*, solution to P_{NC} instead of $P_{SC}(y)$ (with only the constraints (1-4)). Thus, P^* would satisfy necessary capacity conditions that any feasible plan must satisfy anyway.

In the next section, we propose an iterative procedure in which, at each iteration. a better *feasible* plan is calculated, *i.e.*, a procedure that generates a monotone non-increasing sequence of costs. We also prove that this sequence eventually converges to some particular plan, a locally optimal solution to the global problem.

III.4.2   An Iterative Procedure

III.4.2.1   Introduction

Here, we present an **iterative** procedure ([Lasserre 92]) to obtain better results than with the **one-pass** procedure described in the previous Section. This iterative procedure **alternates** between:

- solving a planning problem $P_{SC}(y)$ for a fixed sequence y.

- solving a standard job-shop scheduling problem for a fixed plan P (*i.e.*, the operations o_{ijkt} of jobs associated with P have well-defined fixed processing times)

In standard approaches, the planning models include aggregate capacity constraints of the type mentionned in Section III.2.2. As already noticed, nothing guarantees that the resulting production plan is feasible, *i.e.*, that there exists at least one schedule compatible with that plan.

In our approach, the capacity (or feasibility) constraints in $P_{SC}(y)$ ensure that at each iteration of the procedure, the plan solution to $P_{SC}(y)$ is **feasible** since there exists at least one schedule (using the sequence y) that achieves that plan.

III.4.2.2   The Procedure

Assume that an initial sequence y_0 is given. This choice of y_0 may be arbitrary or as in Section III.4.1. At iteration k of the procedure, given the sequence y_k, let $P^k = (X^k, I^k)$ be an optimal solution to $P_{SC}(y_k)$. The iterative procedure is as follows:

- Step 0: **Initialization Step:** Set $k := 0$, $g_{-1} := +\infty$, and *list* := $\emptyset$.

- Step 1: **Planning Problem:** Solve $P_{SC}(y_k)$.
  If $g_k = g(P^k) < g_{k-1}$ then *list* := y_k.
  If $g_k = g(P^k) = g_{k-1}$ then *list* := *list* $\cup y_k$.

  Let $R(y_k, P^k) := \{0_{ijkt} \in L : t_{ijkt} + p^u_{ijkt}.X^k_{it} = \sum_{l=1}^t c_l\}$ be the set of **active** (or **tight**) capacity constraints (9) in $P_{SC}(y_k)$.
  If $R(y_k, P^k) \equiv \emptyset$, then **STOP**, else go to Step 2.

- Step 2: **Scheduling Problem:** Find a sequence $y \notin list$ such that:

  $$t_{ijkt} + p^u_{ijkt}.X^k_{it} \leq \sum_{l=1}^t c_l, \quad \forall o_{ijkt} \in L.$$

  $$t_{ijkt} + p^u_{ijkt}.X^k_{it} < \sum_{l=1}^t c_l, \text{ for at least some operation } o^0_{ijkt} \in R(y_k, P^k).$$

  If there is no such sequence then go to Step 3 else set $k := k + 1$; $y_k := y$ and go Step 1.

- Step 3: **Scheduling Problem:** Find a sequence $y \notin list$ such that:

  $$t_{ijkt} + p^u_{ijkt}.X^k_{it} \leq \sum_{l=1}^t c_l, \quad \forall o_{ijkt} \in L \text{ and.}$$

  $$t_{ijkt} + p^u_{ijkt}.X^k_{it} = \sum_{l=1}^t c_l, \quad \forall o_{ijkt} \in R(y_k, P^k).$$

  If there is no such sequence then **STOP**, else set $k := k + 1$; $y_k := y$ and go to Step 1.

In Step 1, P^k is an optimal plan with respect to the sequence y_k.

In Step 2, the goal is to find a sequence y better for the plan P^k than the sequence y_k. It suffices to search for a sequence y such that some active capacity constraint in $P_{SC}(y_k)$ is not active any more in $P_{SC}(y)$. Indeed, P^k is **still feasible** for this new sequence y and the capacity constraint being not tight any more, it is then possible to improve P^k (at least slightly) and thus decrease the cost.

When in Step 2, a new sequence y has not been found, all the sequences y compatible with P^k generate the same set of active capacity constraints (at P^k) in $P_{SC}(y)$. However, P^k may not be an optimal solution for some $P_{SC}(y)$. Step 3 explores those sequences y. *List* is a standard device to avoid cycling in the procedure.

Remark III.3

In the case where set-up times are taken into account, we must include the Boolean variables y_{it} in $P_{SC}(y_k)$. Step 1 is more difficult since now $P_{SC}(y_k)$ is a mixed-integer *Linear Program instead of a standard Linear Program in continuous variables. However, apart from that, the procedure is similar.*

One may easily check that the sequence of plans $\{P^k\}_k$ generated by the iterative procedure is such that $\{g(P^k)\}_k$ is a monotone non-increasing sequence and since g is bounded from below ($g \geq 0$), $\{g(P^k)\}_k$ converges to g^*. This convergence is analyzed in Section III.4.2.4.

III.4.2.3   The Scheduling Problem

In Steps 2 and 3 of the procedure, one tries to find a sequence y such that at least one of the *active* capacity constraints (9) in $P_{SC}(y_k)$ for an operation $o_{ijkt} \in L$ is not active any more in $P_{SC}(y)$. Actually, the constraints (9) in $P_{SC}(y)$ correspond to due date satisfaction constraints in the scheduling problem.

Thus, the problem of finding such a sequence y reduces to a standard job-shop scheduling problem with due date constraints and maximum lateness criterion L_{max}.

However, via a simple transformation, this problem reduces in turn to a job-shop scheduling problem with the makespan criterion C_{max}. It suffices to introduce *fictitious arcs* on each operation $o_{ijkt} \in L$ in the disjunctive graph of the scheduling problem (see Chapter IV, Section IV.2.1 for more details). The length l_{it} of a fictitious arc is equal to the length of the horizon H minus the due date of the operation $o_{ijkt} \in L$, i.e.,

$$l_{it} = \sum_{l=1}^{T} c_l - \sum_{l=1}^{t} c_l = \sum_{l=t+1}^{T} c_l \quad (0 \ if \ t = T).$$

Thus, with these fictitious arcs, we can use any of the various algorithms to minimize the makespan in a job-shop.

We used the Modified Shifting Bottleneck (MSB) procedure, presented in Chapter II, Section II.4, based on the procedure proposed by [Adams *et al.* 88]. In Step 2, the length of a fictitious arc is l_{it}, $\forall o_{ijkt} \in L$ ($o_{ijkt} \neq o_{ijkt}^0$), and $l_{it} + \delta$ for the operations o_{ijkt}^0 selected (δ being a small positive scalar).

Moreover, admissibility of a sequence (see Remark III.1) is taken into account in the algorithm by introducing release dates $\sum_{l=1}^{t-1} c_l - p_{ijkt}^t$ for all the operations $o_{ijkt} \in L$.

If there exists a sequence y in Step 2, its corresponding makespan in the modified problem is less than $\sum_{l=1}^{T} c_l + \delta$, whereas the makespan of y_k is larger than this value.

Therefore, in the Modified Shifting Bottleneck procedure, it is not necessary to reach an optimal sequence. It suffices to stop as soon as the makespan is less than $\sum_{l=1}^{T} c_l + \delta$.

Theoretically, it may happen that we find a sequence y with a makespan $\sum_{l=1}^{T} c_l + \delta'$, and $\delta' < \delta$. The plan P^k would not be feasible for y since at least one of the capacity constraint is violated of δ'. In this case one cannot guarantee any more that the plan P^{k+1} computed in solving $P_{SC}(y)$ at iteration $k + 1$ has a smaller cost (however the eventual increase in cost would be small since δ' is small).

Actually, as Y is a finite set, there exists a sufficiently small $\delta > 0$ such that any solution y with makespan less than $\sum_{l=1}^{T} c_l + \delta$, is such that its makespan is in fact less than $\sum_{l=1}^{T} c_l$. In other words, all the capacity constraints are satisfied.

However, the scheduling algorithm being only a *heuristic*, there is no guarantee that we actually find such a sequence even if it exists. Therefore, with a *heuristic*, we cannot guarantee a monotone decrease of the cost. The iterative pocedure described earlier must be understood as an *ideal* procedure.

Thus, for implementation purposes, Step 2 and 3 are replaced by:

- <u>Step 2</u>: **Scheduling Problem:** Find a sequence y which minimizes the makespan in the scheduling problem presented above.
  Set $k := k + 1$; $y_k := y$ and go to Step 1.

Also, in Step 1, we stop when the cost does not decrease any more, or after a pre-specified number of iterations.

This Step 2 is certainly time consuming, at least for large size problems if an efficient heuristic is to be used. However, it is worth noticing that at each iteration, the plan is **feasible** so that the procedure can be stopped at any iteration. The **one-pass** procedure can be a preliminary step.

Remark III.4
list *is used to avoid cycling if the cost remains constant for some iterations. However, in practice, we do not use* list *since a non trivial modification of the scheduling heuristic is required to avoid computing a sequence already selected at a previous iteration. The procedure is stopped as soon as $g_k = g_{k-1}$ in Step 1 of iteration k.*

III.4.2.4   Convergence Properties

To analyze the *quality* of the production plan generated by the iterative procedure, we must compare with the solution obtained in solving the global problem P_{NSC}.

We show below that the *ideal* procedure stops at a locally optimal solution and in a finite number of iterations.

Theorem III.1
The (ideal) iterative procedure, with or without set-up times, stops in a finite number of iterations with a terminal sequence y^* and a production plan $P^* = (X^*, I^*)$. Moreover, P^* is a locally optimal solution of the global problem P_{NSC}.

Proof: Let us first prove that the procedure stops after a finite number of iterations. Suppose not. As the number of admissible sequences in Y is finite, there necessarily exists a sequence y^* that is generated infinitely often in a subsequence. Let $k' > k + |Y|$ (where $|Y|$ stands for the number of elements in Y) with $y_{k'} = y_k = y^*$. The sequence $\{g_k\}$ being non-increasing, we must have $g_k = g_{k'} = g_l$ for all $k \leq l \leq k'$. We must then conclude that, at every iteration between k and k', a *new* sequence is included in *list* in Step 1 of the procedure. But then $|list| \geq k' - k \geq |Y|$, a contradiction. Therefore the procedure stops in a finite number of steps with terminal sequence y^* and production plan $P^* = (X^*, I^*)$.

We now show that P^* is a locally optimal solution to P_{NSC}. The procedure stops either at Step 1 with $R(y^*, P^*) \equiv \emptyset$, or at Step 2 or 3 with $R(y^*, P^*) \neq \emptyset$.

Assume that P^* is not a locally optimal solution to P_{NSC}. Then, there exists a sequence $\{y_k\}_k$ and a sequence $\{P^k\}_k = \{(X^k, I^k)\}_k$ of *feasible* production plans, satisfying the capacity constraints in $P_{NSC}(y_k)$ (or $P_{SC}^{tp}(y_k)$), and converging to P^*, with associated costs $g(P^k) < g^* = g(P^*)$, $\forall k$.

As Y is a finite set, there exists a subsequence $\{y_{k'}\}_{k'}$ (and an associated subsequence $\{P^{k'}\}_{k'}$) such that $y_{k'} = y'$, $\forall k'$. All the starting times $t_{ijkt}^{k'}$ being in the (compact) interval $[0, \sum_{l=1}^{T} c_l]$, one may extract another subsequence $\{y_{k''}\}_{k''}$ (and $\{P^{k''}\}_{k''}$), such that $t_{ijkt}^{k''}$ converges to $t_{ijkt}^{"}$, for all the operations $o_{ijkt} \in N$.

The analysis is slightly different depending on the presence of set-up times.

- **with no set-up time:**
  For k'' sufficiently large, *i.e.* such that the starting times $t_{ijkt}^{k''}$ are sufficiently close to $t_{ijkt}^{"}$, constraints (5) and (7) in $P_{SC}(y')$ satisfied by $(X_{it}^{k''}, t_{ijkt}^{k''}, t_{ij'k't}^{k''}, t_{i'j'kt'}^{k''})$, are also satisfied by $(X_{it}^*, t_{ijkt}^{"}, t_{ij'k't}^{"}, t_{i'j'kt'}^{"})$ (using a simple continuity argument). The same is true for constraints (9) and (10).

- **with set-up times:**
  As long as $X_{it}^* > 0$, the argument is the same as in case of no set-up time. Indeed, the set-up times τ_{ijkt} are constant ($y_{it} = 1$ for $X_{it}^{k''}$ and X_{it}^*). If $X_{it}^* = 0$, then a discontinuity appears in the constraints if $X_{it}^{k''} > 0$. However in this case $X_{it}^{k''} \downarrow X_{it}^*$. Then, constraint (5):

$$t_{ijkt}^{k''} - t_{ij'k't}^{k''} - p_{ij'k't}^u . X_{it}^{k''} - \tau_{ijkt} . y_{it}^{k''} \geq 0$$

$$\Rightarrow t_{ijkt}^{k"} \geq t_{ij'k't}^{k"} + p_{ij'k't}^{u} \cdot X_{it}^{k"} + \tau_{ijkt} \cdot y_{it}^{k"}$$

is necessarily satisfied for $(X_{it}^* = 0, \, y_{it}^* = 0, \, t_{ijkt}^{"} = 0, \, t_{ij'k't}^{"} = 0)$.
The same is true for constraints (7) and (9), more restrictive for $(X_{it}^{k"}, \, y_{it}^{k"},$
$t_{ijkt}^{k"}, \, t_{ij'k't}^{k"})$ than for $(X_{it}^* = 0, \, y_{it}^* = 0, \, t_{ijkt}^{"}, \, t_{ij'k't}^{"})$.

However, constraint (10), independent of y':

$$t_{ijkt}^{k"} \geq \sum_{l=1}^{t-1} c_l - p_{ijkt}^{u} \cdot X_{it}^{k"} - \tau_{ijkt} \cdot y_{it}^{k"}$$

might not be satisfied by $(X_{it}^*, \, y_{it}^*, \, t_{ijkt}^{"})$. But, as $X_{it}^* = 0$, we may always set
$t_{ijkt}^{"}$ to $\sum_{l=1}^{t-1} c_l$ (constraint (10) for $(X_{it}^* = 0, \, y_{it}^* = 0, \, t_{ijkt}^{"}))$ with no effect on the
other constraints, i.e.the starting times of the other operations.

This implies that the plan P^* is feasible for the sequence y'. But then, at Step 2
or 3 of the procedure, this sequence should have eventually been chosen. And at
Step 1, a production plan with a strictly smaller cost would have been generated in
solving $P_{SC}(y')$ (or $P_{SC}^{tp}(y')$), a contradiction with our hypothesis. ♣

III.5   First Computational Results

III.5.1   With no Set-Up Times

We have been unable to find in the literature any example of a procedure computing *simultaneously* a production plan and a schedule compatible with that plan.
Therefore, we have tested our procedure as follows:

- We have chosen a standard scheduling problem in a job-shop with 6 machines
  and 6 jobs described in [Fisher and Thompson 63], that we call the original
  problem. The makespan is known to be 55. In our model, the processing times
  of this original problem become the per unit processing times.

- To each period in the horizon, we set all the demands D_{it} to 1, and the length
  of each period to 55 ($c_1 = c_2 = ... = c_T = 55$). All the set-up times and
  associated set-up costs are set to zero.

Let y^* be the sequence in which, at each period, the jobs are scheduled with
the optimal sequence of the original problem. By using y^*, the production plan
$P^* = (X^*, I^*)$ such that: $X_{it}^* = D_{it} = 1$, and $I_{it}^* = 0 \; \forall i, t$, is achievable with
the sequence y^*, i.e., is feasible. Finally, if the production costs are set to zero
($c_{it}^{pr} = 0, \; \forall i, t$), the plan P^* is a global optimal solution with associated cost $g^* = 0$.

Consequently, starting with an arbitrary sequence, it is desirable that the procedure *ideally* converges to a production plan with a cost close (or equal) to zero.

The data are:

$T = 3, c_1 = c_2 = c_3 = 55$
$D_{it} = 1, i = 1, .., 6; \ t = 1, 2, 3$
$c_{it}^{pr} = 0, c_{it}^+ = 5, c_{it}^- = 50, i = 1, .., 6; \ t = 1, 2, 3$
$\Delta_{it} = 0, i = 1, .., 6; \ t = 1, 2, 3$
$\tau_{ijkt} = 0, o_{ijkt} \in N$

Table III.1 gives the routing of jobs on the machines and the associated processing times in the original problem.

Job	Machine (processing time)					
1	3 (1)	1 (3)	2 (6)	4 (7)	6 (3)	5 (6)
2	2 (8)	3 (5)	5 (10)	6 (10)	1 (10)	4 (4)
3	3 (5)	4 (4)	6 (8)	1 (9)	2 (1)	5 (7)
4	2 (5)	1 (5)	3 (5)	4 (3)	5 (8)	6 (9)
5	3 (9)	2 (3)	5 (5)	6 (4)	1 (3)	4 (1)
6	2 (3)	4 (3)	6 (9)	1 (10)	5 (4)	3 (1)

Table III.1: 6-6 job-shop scheduling problem

To test the procedure, we have arbitrarily chosen 6 different initial production plans (*i.e.*, 6 vectors X), all far away from the optimal plan X^*. The initial sequence is generated in solving the scheduling problem with the initial plan. Results are displayed in Table III.2 where the *cost at the first iteration* is the cost associated to that plan.

For instance, in Problem 1, the cost at the first iteration is 1069.1. At iteration 2, the production plan is:

$(0.00, 0.81, 0.48, 0.86, 1.20, 0.55)$ at the first period,
$(2.30, 1.19, 1.13, 0.69, 0.80, 0.89)$ at the second period, and
$(0.70, 0.85, 1.39, 1.45, 1.00, 0.39)$ at the third and last period.

The cost associated to this plan is 253.6. Then, the cost decreases monotonically (52.0, 10.1, 7.9), and the optimal solution X^* is eventually reached at iteration 6. In Problem 3, the cost also decreases monotonically but does not converge to zero. However, the plan is very close to X^*.

One may observe that, in these small size examples for which the scheduling algorithm used is very efficient, the optimal solution X^* has been found three times out of six and, when not found, the plan reached is very close to X^*.

Pb	Initial Plan						Cost 1st it.	Final Plan						Cost	Nb iter.
1	10.0	0.4	15.0	3.0	0.6	6.0	1069.1			X^*				0	6
	2.0	10.0	10.0	0.5	0.4	0.2									
	8.0	1.0	3.0	0.7	0.8	5.0									
2	0.6	4.0	3.0	0.6	3.0	4.0	291.3			X^*				0	7
	5.0	0.7	0.5	3.0	0.4	2.0									
	1.0	3.0	0.7	0.8	2.0	0.6									
3	4.0	3.0	0.6	3.0	4.0	0.6	799.2	1.00	1.00	0.92	1.00	1.00	1.00	4.0	5
	0.7	0.5	3.0	0.4	2.0	5.0		1.00	1.00	1.08	1.00	1.00	1.00		
	3.0	7.0	2.0	2.0	0.6	1.0		1.00	1.00	1.00	1.00	1.00	1.00		
4	2.0	3.0	3.0	0.6	0.5	0.8	1514.1			X^*				0	9
	3.0	0.5	0.3	3.0	0.8	0.6									
	0.5	0.9	1.0	5.0	4.0	4.0									
5	0.4	3.0	3.0	0.4	3.0	0.8	344.6	1.00	0.95	0.87	1.00	1.00	1.00	9.0	6
	3.0	0.5	1.0	3.0	0.8	3.0		1.00	1.05	1.13	1.00	1.00	1.00		
	5.0	3.0	0.4	0.8	0.7	4.0		1.00	1.00	1.00	1.00	1.00	1.00		
6	2.0	0.7	1.0	0.8	3.0	2.0	454.9	1.00	0.95	0.87	1.00	1.00	1.00	9.0	6
	2.0	0.6	0.4	3.0	0.6	5.0		1.00	1.05	1.13	1.00	1.00	1.00		
	0.5	4.0	0.7	1.0	0.8	0.6		1.00	1.00	1.00	1.00	1.00	1.00		

Table III.2: Fixed routing and processing times; no set-up time; different initial plans

III.5.2   With Set-Up Times

We consider the same problem as in the previous Section. The only difference is the set-up times introduced by modifying the data as follows: $\tau_{ijkt} = 0.1 p_{ijk}$ and $p_{ijkt}^u = 0.9 p_{ijk}$ $\forall o_{ijkt} \in N$, where p_{ijk} is the set-up time of operation o_{ijk} in the *original* problem.

As in the previous section, the production plan P^* such that $X_{it}^* = 1$, $\forall i$, t is still optimal with optimal associated cost $g^* = 0$ (since $c_{it}^{pr} = 0$, $\forall i$, t).

The results are displayed in Table III.3 and the interpretation is the same as before. The same initial plans have been used. Here also, in three examples out of six the optimal solution X^* is reached in few iterations. When not found, the final plan is still very close to X^*.

III.5.3   Other Computational Results

First, we have kept the same routing as in Table III.1 ([Fisher and Thompson 63]), but we have randomly generated the processing times with a uniform probability distribution on the interval $[1, 10]$. The length of the period is also constant on the horizon, and still equal to the minimum makespan of the generated schedul-

Pb	Initial Plan						Cost 1st it.	Final Plan						Cost	Nb iter.
1	10.0	0.4	15.0	3.0	0.6	6.0	835.0			X^*				0	5
	2.0	10.0	10.0	0.5	0.4	0.2									
	8.0	1.0	3.0	0.7	0.8	5.0									
2	0.6	4.0	3.0	0.6	3.0	4.0	340.1	1.00	1.00	0.91	1.00	1.00	1.00	4.5	4
	5.0	0.7	0.5	3.0	0.4	2.0		1.00	1.00	1.09	1.00	1.00	1.00		
	1.0	3.0	0.7	0.8	2.0	0.6		1.00	1.00	1.00	1.00	1.00	1.00		
3	4.0	3.0	0.6	3.0	4.0	0.6	622.1	1.00	1.00	0.91	1.00	1.00	1.00	4.5	7
	0.7	0.5	3.0	0.4	2.0	5.0		1.00	1.00	1.09	1.00	1.00	1.00		
	3.0	7.0	2.0	2.0	0.6	1.0		1.00	1.00	1.00	1.00	1.00	1.00		
4	2.0	3.0	3.0	0.6	0.5	0.8	351.9			X^*				0	8
	3.0	0.5	0.3	3.0	0.8	0.6									
	0.5	0.9	1.0	5.0	4.0	4.0									
5	0.4	3.0	3.0	0.4	3.0	0.8	368.0			X^*				0	12
	3.0	0.5	1.0	3.0	0.8	3.0									
	5.0	3.0	0.4	0.8	0.7	4.0									
6	2.0	0.7	1.0	0.8	3.0	2.0	358.1	1.00	0.81	1.00	1.00	1.00	1.00	9.5	6
	2.0	0.6	0.4	3.0	0.6	5.0		1.00	1.19	1.00	1.00	1.00	1.00		
	0.5	4.0	0.7	1.0	0.8	0.6		1.00	1.00	1.00	1.00	1.00	1.00		

Table III.3: Fixed routing and processing times; set-up times; different initial plans.

ing problem. This minimum makespan is computed by using the Modified Shifting Bottleneck procedure.

The other parameters are not modified and the production plan P^* ($X_{it}^* = 1$, $\forall i$, t) is still optimal with associated cost $g^* = 0$. The results are displayed in Table III.4.

The fixed initial plan is: $\begin{vmatrix} 2.0 & 0.5 & 1.4 & 0.7 & 1.8 & 0.3 \\ 0.2 & 0.7 & 0.7 & 1.9 & 0.1 & 0.8 \\ 0.8 & 1.8 & 0.9 & 0.4 & 1.1 & 1.9 \end{vmatrix}$

This initial plan is the same for the problems in Tables III.4 and III.5. In this last table, processing times, as well as routings, have been randomly generated. Each routing has been randomly chosen with a uniform probability distribution among the 6! = 720 possible routings. The length of the period, constant over the horizon, has also been determined by the Modified Shifting Bottleneck procedure.

In both tables, the global optimal solution has been reached 8 times out of 10 and in the 2 other cases, the final plan is very close to the optimal plan X^*. The reader is referred to [Dauzere-Peres 92] and [Dauzere-Peres and Lasserre 94] for more details.

Pb	Length of the period	Cost 1st it.	Final Plan						Cost	Nb iter.
1	63	670.8	X^*						0	4
2	56	345.0	X^*						0	7
3	60	281.4	X^*						0	3
4	64	87.2	X^*						0	3
5	68	451.8	0.95	1.00	1.00	1.00	1.00	1.00	2.50	6
			1.05	1.00	1.00	1.00	1.00	1.00		
			1.00	1.00	1.00	1.00	1.00	1.00		
6	60	435.2	X^*						0	4
7	61	91.3	X^*						0	4
8	52	221.0	X^*						0	7
9	61	128.4	X^*						0	3
10	55	527.2	1.00	1.00	1.00	0.88	1.00	1.00	6.0	4
			1.00	1.00	1.00	1.12	1.00	1.00		
			1.00	1.00	1.00	1.00	1.00	1.00		

Table III.4: Fixed routing and initial plan; no set-up time; random processing times.

Pb	Length of the periode	Cost 1st it.	Final Plan						Cost	Nb iter.
1	53	621.2	X^*						0	6
2	56	126.5	X^*						0	4
3	59	91.0	1.00	0.86	1.00	1.00	1.00	1.00	7.0	6
			1.00	1.14	1.00	1.00	1.00	1.00		
			1.00	1.00	1.00	1.00	1.00	1.00		
4	58	620.4	X^*						0	5
5	56	366.0	X^*						0	5
6	49	301.7	1.00	1.00	1.00	0.94	1.00	1.00	3.0	11
			1.00	1.00	1.00	1.06	1.00	1.00		
			1.00	1.00	1.00	1.00	1.00	1.00		
7	57	563.7	X^*						0	7
8	62	57.9	X^*						0	4
9	62	513.4	X^*						0	4
10	53	287.2	X^*						0	4

Table III.5: Fixed initial plan; no set-up time; random routing and processing times.

III.6 Conclusion

We have first presented several ways to integrate detailed capacity constraints induced by a job-shop in a planning model. These detailed capacity constraints are completely described via necessary and sufficient conditions, or partially described via either necessary conditions or sufficient conditions.

Based on the latter conditions, two procedures have been proposed to solve the integrated planning and scheduling problem. The *one-pass* procedure is simple, fast, and yields a **feasible** production plan. The iterative (**multi-pass**) procedure improves the first one, and alternates between solving a planning problem with a **fixed** sequence of jobs on the machines, and solving a standard scheduling problem for a **fixed** production plan.

In contrast to other methods, each generated production plan is **feasible**, *i.e.*, there exists at least one feasible schedule to achieve that production plan. It is worth noting that **no schedule is imposed** to the decision maker. Along with the production plan, a sequence is **proposed** and ensures that the production plan is feasible. After the production plan has been computed, any other scheduling procedure can be applied.

*

*   *

Chapter IV

Various Resolution Strategies

IV.1   Introduction

In this chapter, we describe several ways of implementing the iterative procedure presented in Chapter III.

We present two policies for multi-period scheduling: the global policy and the period by period policy. For each of them, two scheduling algorithms — the Modified Shifting Bottleneck (MSB) procedure and a Priority Rule-based Dispatching (PRD) heuristic (see Chapter II) — are implemented. Each case is tested on a sample of 7 problems (also used in Chapter V) in order to see the impact of the scheduling policies and the scheduling algorithms on the efficiency of the iterative procedure. Other multi-period scheduling policies are also discussed in Section IV.2.4.

Section IV.3 briefly shows how the procedure reacts when priorities are fixed on the fulfillment of the demands of some products, *i.e.*, when the cost coefficients discriminate between products and periods. The planning level is able to drive the scheduling algorithm so that demand is satisfied according to the priorities in the coefficients.

Finally, the last part of this chapter is devoted to the implementation of the iterative procedure on a rolling horizon. Depending on the multi-period scheduling policy chosen, some changes are necessary.

IV.2   Two   Multi-Period   Scheduling   Policies

In this section, we consider two different policies for solving the multi-period scheduling problem:

- In the **global** policy, the general problem is solved without any particular condition, *i.e.*, all the jobs J_{it} ($\forall i, t$) are considered simultaneously.

- In the **period by period** policy, a job J_{it} ($\in J^t$) can only be processed on a machine k if all the previous jobs in $J^{t'}$ ($\forall t' < t$) have already been sequenced on k.

The second policy has been developed because solving the global problem is time consuming with the Modified Shifting Bottleneck (MSB) procedure. Moreover, it is sometimes impossible to consider the global policy in some industrial contexts.

Each policy has been tested with two scheduling methods: the Modified Shifting Bottleneck (MSB) procedure and a Priority Rule-based Dispatching (PRD) heuristic (see Chapter II for details on both methods). The first method gives lower makespans than the second one, and we will observe the impact on the iterative procedure. However, PRD is easier to implement and permits to handle large scale problems.

Again, we chose the famous job-shop problem with 6 jobs and 6 machines given in [Fisher and Thompson 63], replicated on 3 periods (*i.e.*, the structure is repeated at each period, see Figure IV-1 below). In our sample, demands in the first period have been randomly generated in the interval $[2, 10]$, and in the interval $[2, 25]$ in the second and the third period.

The parameters in $P_{SC}(y)$ have the following values:

available time units per period, $c_1 = c_2 = c_3 = 550$;
initial inventories, $I_{i0} = 0$, $i = 1..6$;
costs, $c_{it}^+ = 1$, $c_{it}^- = 10$, and $c_{it}^{pr} = 0$, $i = 1..6$, $t = 1..3$.

For reasons that will be explained in the sequel, the procedure does not converge monotonically. This is why we fixed a maximum number of iterations (10), and kept the best solution (the one with the lowest cost g_f). We computed the reduction between the initial cost (g_i), obtained at the end of the first iteration, and the final cost (g_f), associated to the best solution. The relative improvement, in %, is equal to $1 - (g_f / g_i)$. The number of iterations needed to find g_f is also given in the tables (column *Nb iter.*).

IV.2.1   The Global Scheduling Policy

With this policy, all the operations are scheduled in a *global* way. That is to say, in a schedule, an operation of a job of period t can be processed before an operation of a job of a previous period $t' < t$.

As shown in the example of Figure IV-1, no matter the period of their jobs, all the operations that must be processed on machine 1 are considered simultaneously. For example, operation o_{1112} can be sequenced before operations o_{2211} or o_{3211}, in an optimal schedule. The Gantt chart of Figure IV-2 shows a schedule in which the

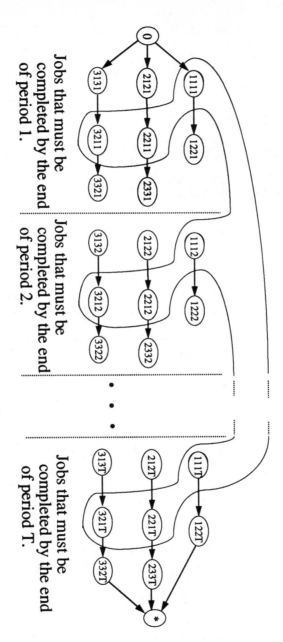

Figure IV-1: Global scheduling policy.

available time on machine 3, between operations o_{3131} and o_{2331}, allows operation o_{3132} (of a job of the second period) to be scheduled in the first period.

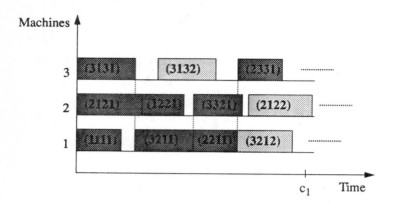

Figure IV-2: Gantt chart in the global scheduling policy.

With global scheduling, the jobs differ by their respective due dates, *i.e.*, J_{it} must be finished before $c_1 + .. + c_t$. Actually, the scheduling problem consists of minimizing the maximum lateness L_{max}. If $L_{max} = 0$, then every job is completed before its due date (*i.e.*, is *on time*). This problem can be reduced to the minimization of the makespan C_{max} (the maximum completion time), by adding *fictitious* arcs between the last operation of each job ($\in L$) and the finish operation $*$. The length of the fictitious arc associated to J_{it} is equal to the processing time of the last operation of J_{it}, plus the difference between the length of the horizon ($H = c_1 + c_2 + ... + c_T$) and the due date of J_{it} (see Figure IV-3).

Instead of arcs, one can add *fictitious* nodes (operations) which do not use any ressource, and of processing time equal to the sum of the lengths of the remaining periods (see Figure IV-4).

IV.2.1.1   The   Modified   Shifting   Bottleneck   (MSB) Procedure

With the global scheduling policy, no matter the period, all the operations that must be processed on machine k are considered in the One-Machine Sequencing (OMS) problems related to machine k. Adding the fictitious arcs affects the delivery times (q_i) computed before solving every One-Machine Sequencing problem (see Chapter II).

Table IV.1 presents the results on the sample of 7 problems. The average computing time per iteration (*i.e.*, determination of the sequence y and the solution of $P_{SC}(y)$) is 25.3 seconds on a Sun 4.1 workstation,

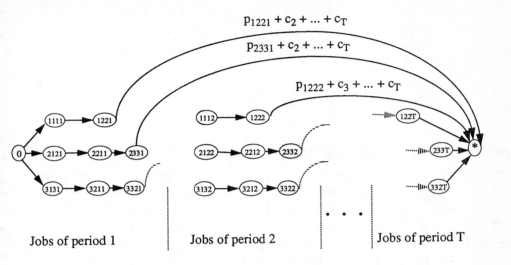

Figure IV-3: Introduction of fictitious arcs.

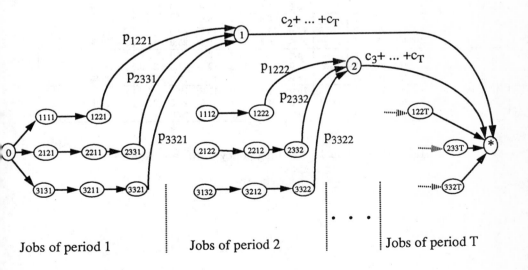

Figure IV-4: Introduction of fictitious nodes.

Pb	Initial plan - Demands						g_i	Final plan						g_f $100(1-g_f/g_i)$	Nb iter.
1	7	7	10	3	7	9	82.0	11.3	7.0	10.3	7.9	7.5	9.4		8
	15	6	20	20	17	10		11.7	6.0	19.7	15.1	16.5	9.6	27.9	
	22	12	21	19	11	14		21.0	11.4	19.9	19.0	11.0	14.0	66 %	
2	4	6	8	7	3	9	106.4	5.6	6.0	10.9	7.0	3.0	9.0		3
	12	10	23	21	10	17		10.4	10.0	20.1	21.0	10.0	17.0	75.7	
	19	12	16	18	23	13		19.0	5.1	16.0	17.8	23.0	13.0	29 %	
3	5	3	5	2	9	9	108.7	5.0	5.8	5.0	4.3	9.0	10.6		8
	11	19	10	24	12	11		11.0	15.6	14.5	21.7	12.0	9.4	17.6	
	12	8	19	23	11	22		12.0	8.6	14.5	23.0	11.0	22.0	84 %	
4	8	4	3	7	10	3	419.0	11.7	1.3	3.0	7.0	10.0	9.5		3
	16	7	23	23	11	21		12.3	9.7	22.9	21.0	11.0	14.5	218.5	
	10	17	20	17	19	21		10.0	8.2	20.1	19.0	19.0	13.9	48 %	
								9.8	1.6	3.9	8.4	10.0	8.6		9
								14.2	9.4	22.1	21.6	11.0	16.5	177.2	
								10.0	5.5	18.6	17.0	19.0	18.6	58 %	
5	4	8	4	5	7	5	434.3	4.0	8.0	8.7	5.0	7.0	10.8		4
	17	21	24	11	20	22		17.0	14.8	18.4	13.2	20.0	16.2	130.8	
	22	2	13	16	25	11		22.0	6.8	13.9	10.5	25.0	11.0	70 %	
6	3	5	7	2	3	8	23.2	3.0	5.0	7.2	2.0	3.0	8.0		2
	21	14	13	19	21	22		21.0	14.0	12.8	19.0	21.0	22.0	0.3	
	14	10	17	18	16	10		14.0	10.0	17.0	18.0	16.0	10.0	99 %	
7	10	9	9	9	10	6	441.4	10.0	9.4	9.9	11.2	10.0	7.0		8
	23	2	10	10	21	23		23.0	4.1	9.1	7.8	21.0	22.0	23.1	
	12	20	13	15	20	15		12.0	15.9	13.0	15.0	20.0	15.0	95 %	

Table IV.1: Global scheduling policy; MSB procedure.

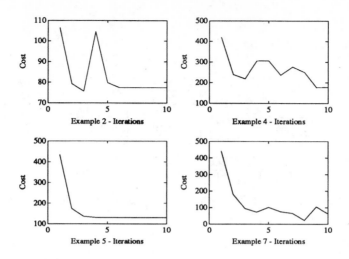

Figure IV-5: Global scheduling policy; MSB procedure.

In all the problems, the procedure finds a *good* solution after few iterations. The gain varies from 29% in Problem 2, to 90% in Problems 6 and 7. In Problem 4, the cost strongly decreases after 3 iterations, but we must wait until the 9th iteration to obtain a lower cost. The behavior of the procedure is rather erratic, as it can be observed on Figure IV-5.

The sudden jumps of the cost in the procedure are due to the fact that the MSB procedure is only a heuristic. Let P_k (cost g_k) be the solution of $P_{SC}(y_k)$ at iteration k. When solving the scheduling problem, we may determine a sequence y_{k+1} which is worse than y_k (the cost of $P_{SC}(y_{k+1})$ is greater than the cost of $P_{SC}(y_k)$) since we use a heuristic. And in $P_{SC}(y_{k+1})$, since P_k is not feasible anymore, we cannot ensure a decrease of the cost. With the ideal procedure, this phenomenon could not occurre.

There is a way to avoid this problem with the MSB procedure. In the first step of the iterative procedure, the sequence y_1 is normally computed. However, the next sequence y_2 is determined by sending y_1 directly in the last re-optimization step of the MSB procedure (see details of the MSB procedure in Chapter II). y_2 will differ from y_1 only if it enables the makespan C_{max} to decrease. Thus, P_1 will remain feasible for y_2, and the cost of the plan P_2 is lower than or equal to the one of P_1, $g_2 \leq g_1$. By repeating this at each step, we prevent the cost from increasing. Table IV.2 presents the results obtained with this modification.

The average computing time per iteration is 15.1 seconds on a SUN 4 workstation. The curves in Figure IV-6 show that the procedure now converges very fast to a

Pb	g_i	g_f	$100(1-g_f/g_i)$	Nb iter.
1	82.0	43.9	46 %	2
2	106.4	91.6	14 %	2
3	108.7	108.7	0 %	1
4	419.0	306.3	27 %	6
5	434.3	356.8	18 %	3
6	23.2	19.4	16 %	2
7	441.4	201.1	54 %	7

Table IV.2: Global scheduling policy; MSB procedure with modification.

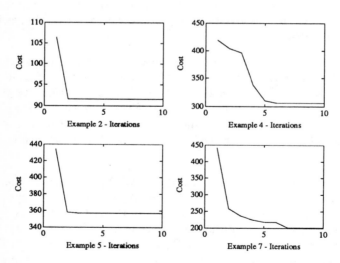

Figure IV-6: Global scheduling policy; MSB procedure with modification.

stable solution. Actually, in Problem 3, the cost never decreases. In 5 out of 7 problems only 3 iterations at most are needed to find the best solution.

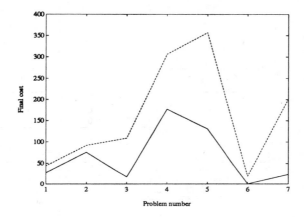

— Final cost without the modification.
- - Final cost with the modification.

Figure IV-7: Global scheduling policy; MSB procedure. Final costs with and without the modification.

However, the final costs obtained with the modification are larger than those obtained without the modification (see Figure IV-7). The improvement is never larger than 54%, obtained in problem 7.

It seems that the jumps of the costs induced by the computation of a wrong sequence at the scheduling level, allows the procedure to leave a *stable* solution, to move to another one. In a sense, temporary increasing of the cost is profitable. One can relate this observation to the broader context of local search algorithms. In Simulated Annealing (see [Van Laarhoven *et al.* 92], or Chapter II), augmentations of the cost are allowed under some conditions in order to ensure convergence (in probability) to a global minimum.

IV.2.1.2 A Priority Rule-Based Dispatching (PRD) Heuristic

When the multi-period scheduling problem is solved with the PRD heuristic, adding the *fictitious* arcs enables the MWKR (Most WorK Remaining) rule to be used with success. Actually, using MWKR is equivalent to using the SLACK rule, where the priority is given to the operation of the job with the smallest due date. Classical rules, such as SPT (Shortest Processing Time), LPT (Longest Processing Time), or FIFO (First In First Out) give bad results. The large differences between due dates of jobs that share a common machine, are not taken into account in these rules.

Pb	Initial plan - Demands						g_i	Final plan						g_f $100(1-g_f/g_i)$	Nb iter.
1	7	7	10	3	7	9		10.0	7.0	13.8	9.0	7.0	9.0		
	15	6	20	20	17	10	190.1	14.4	6.0	16.2	14.0	19.3	10.0	100.6	3
	22	12	21	19	11	14		19.5	12.0	12.7	19.0	8.7	14.0	47 %	
2	4	6	8	7	3	9		6.9	6.7	12.3	8.4	3.0	9.0		
	12	10	23	21	10	17	303.9	9.1	5.8	16.4	19.6	10.7	17.0	182.0	4
	19	12	16	18	23	13		19.0	14.3	14.6	18.0	17.0	11.7	40 %	
3	5	3	5	2	9	9		5.0	6.7	8.8	8.9	9.0	10.7		
	11	19	10	24	12	11	460.7	11.0	15.3	11.4	19.7	12.0	17.2	50.8	4
	12	8	19	23	11	22		12.0	8.0	13.8	18.5	11.0	14.1	89 %	
								5.0	5.9	5.0	7.4	9.0	10.3		
								11.0	16.1	13.3	18.6	12.0	14.0	39.3	9
								12.0	8.0	15.7	20.8	11.0	17.7	91 %	
4	8	4	3	7	10	3		9.7	4.8	11.4	10.0	10.0	10.4		
	16	7	23	23	11	21	401.2	14.4	6.2	14.6	17.0	11.4	13.6	269.7	9
	10	17	20	17	19	21		10.0	8.9	20.1	20.0	7.9	18.1	33 %	
5	4	8	4	5	7	5		10.1	8.2	7.3	6.8	7.3	11.3		
	17	21	24	11	20	22	807.3	10.9	11.4	13.9	9.2	19.7	15.7	239.9	5
	22	2	13	16	25	11		22.0	11.4	16.8	13.1	25.0	11.0	70 %	
6	3	5	7	2	3	8		3.0	5.0	8.2	7.2	7.4	8.0		
	21	14	13	19	21	22	11.2	21.0	14.0	12.2	13.8	16.6	22.0	11.2	1
	14	10	17	18	16	10		14.0	10.0	16.6	18.0	16.0	10.0	0 %	
7	10	9	9	9	10	6		10.1	6.5	9.9	10.0	10.0	11.0		
	23	2	10	10	21	23	142.3	22.7	5.8	7.6	9.0	23.2	18.0	142.3	1
	12	20	13	15	20	15		12.2	12.8	14.5	12.8	17.0	15.0	0 %	

Table IV.3: Global scheduling policy; PRD heuristic.

The results are given in Table IV.3. The average computing time per iteration is 17.1 seconds. This figure is hardly comparable with the one obtained using the MSB procedure since, even for large problems, the computing time for the PRD heuristic is still within acceptable limits (the computational complexity is linear in the number of operations), which is not the case for MSB, in particular for a large number of machines. Except for the last two problems, the cost has decreased significantly. The gain is greater than 30% in the first five problems.

The curves of Figure IV-8 show the oscillation of the cost with the iterations. Abrupt growths of the cost have the same explanation as in the previous section.

IV.2.1.3   Comparison between the Two Scheduling Methods

Clearly, the quality of the final solution strongly depends on the quality of the procedure used at the scheduling level. A *good* scheduling algorithm must lead to a less erratic behavior of the method. The frequency of the jumps in the cost can be reduced, and the height of these jumps as well.

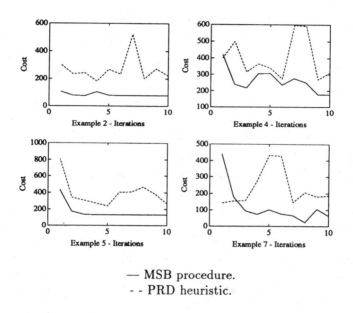

— MSB procedure.
- - PRD heuristic.

Figure IV-8: Global scheduling policy; MSB procedure and PRD heuristic.

This remark is confirmed in our sample (Figure IV-8). The behavior of the iterative procedure is better when MSB is used at the scheduling level. Figure IV-9 shows that the best results are obtained when the scheduling algorithm which gives the lowest makespan is used.

However, in the next section, we shall see that, more than the scheduling algorithm, the choice of the multi-period scheduling policy seems crucial.

IV.2.2   The Period by Period Scheduling Policy

Global scheduling with the MSB procedure requires CPU-times which rapidly increase in the number of machines and the number of jobs. The latter is in turn a function of the number of periods T.

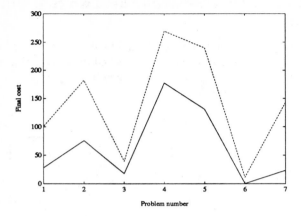

— Final cost with MSB procedure.
- - Final cost with PRD heuristic.

Figure IV-9: Global scheduling policy. Final costs with the two scheduling methods.

To reduce these computing times, we developed an algorithm in which the whole problem is decoupled into T sub-problems. Jobs of differents periods are considered separately (period decoupling). First, the jobs in period 1 ($\in J^1$) are sequenced, then those in period 2 ($\in J^2$), and so forth. An operation o_{ijkt} can only be processed on the machine k if all the operations $o_{i'j'kt'}$ ($t' < t$) have been processed on k. As shown in Figure IV-10, the operations that have to be processed on machine 1, and corresponding to jobs of the first period, must be sequenced before the operations which belong to jobs of the other periods.

In this case, *fictitious* arcs (or nodes) are useless, because the jobs of a period are scheduled independently from the jobs of the previous or following periods. Nevertheless, it is still possible to begin jobs of period t in a previous period $t' < t$.

Looking back at the Gantt chart of Figure IV-2, in the period by period scheduling policy (Gantt chart of Figure IV-11), operation o_{3132} cannot be scheduled between operations o_{3131} and o_{2331} of jobs of the first period. However, operations o_{1112} and o_{2122} can start before c_1. Actually, o_{1112} can start as soon as all the operations of jobs of the first period (o_{1111}, o_{3211} and o_{2211}) have been processed on machine 1. Similarly for operation o_{2122} on machine 2.

With this policy, the computing time decreases when the MSB procedure is used. However, with a very simple PRD heuristic such as the one we used, the improvement is not obvious since the computing time for solving T one-period problems is the same as for solving the problem globally on the T periods

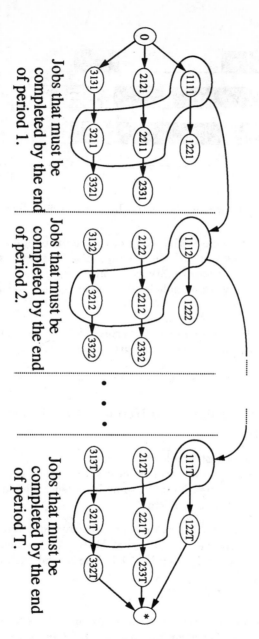

Figure IV-10: Period by period scheduling policy.

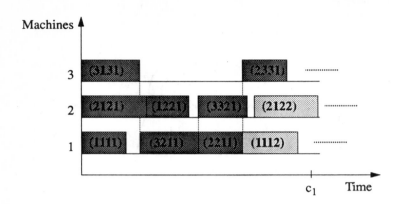

Figure IV-11: Gantt chart in the period by period scheduling policy.

The second reason that supports the study of this multi-period scheduling policy, is that overlapping of jobs of differents periods may not be possible in some manufacturing systems. This impossibility may come from physical constraints of the workshop, but also from working policies decided at higher levels.

Remark IV.1
The set of possible sequences in the period by period scheduling policy is a subset of the one in the global policy, i.e., better results are expected with the latter.

In Section IV.2.3, this remark is illustrated by the numerical experiments.

IV.2.2.1   The   Modified   Shifting   Bottleneck   ₀(MSB) Procedure

Results on the earlier stated test problems are given in Table IV.4. The average computing time per iteration is 14.7 seconds, nearly 10 seconds less than in global scheduling. The cost is still decreasing after some iterations. This decrease ranges from 13% in problem 4, to 60% in problem 6.

In Figure IV-12, we can see that the iterative procedure oscillates a lot. These oscillations have two explanations. The fact that MSB is only a heuristic is a first explanation, already discussed in Section IV.2.1.1. The second explanation is given in the following remark.

Remark IV.2
When the jobs of a period t $(\in J^t)$ are scheduled, the jobs of the previous periods t' $(t' < t)$ are taken into account, but not the jobs of the following periods t' $(t' > t)$, i.e., the procedure is non anticipative (or myopic). Therefore, when minimizing the makespan of jobs in period t, one may degrade the overall makespan.

Pb	Initial plan - Demands						g_i	Final plan						g_f 100(1-g_f/g_i)	Nb iter.
1	7	7	10	3	7	9	143.6	11.0	7.0	13.5	7.2	11.2	9.0	108.1	3
	15	6	20	20	17	10		12.2	7.0	16.5	17.7	12.8	10.0	25 %	
	22	12	21	19	11	14		20.8	7.6	15.6	17.1	11.0	14.0		
2	4	6	8	7	3	9	253.5	7.2	6.4	10.8	10.8	3.7	9.0	205.4	6
	12	10	23	21	10	17		11.1	9.6	18.1	18.0	9.3	13.3	19 %	
	19	12	16	18	23	13		16.7	1.9	18.1	16.7	23.0	14.0		
3	5	3	5	2	9	9	255.6	6.6	5.6	5.4	8.4	9.0	9.1	129.3	10
	11	19	10	24	12	11		16.8	16.4	9.6	17.6	12.0	15.9	49 %	
	12	8	19	23	11	22		4.6	6.1	11.7	21.6	11.0	17.0		
4	8	4	3	7	10	3	354.6	7.1	4.2	8.3	12.2	10.9	10.2	309.4	3
	16	7	23	23	11	21		16.9	6.3	17.3	16.3	13.5	13.8	13 %	
	10	17	20	17	19	21		10.0	11.7	8.0	15.6	15.6	17.0		
5	4	8	4	5	7	5	518.5	9.8	9.4	13.7	5.0	12.3	9.8	309.3	8
	17	21	24	11	20	22		17.7	11.3	13.3	11.8	15.1	11.1	40 %	
	22	2	13	16	25	11		15.5	4.9	9.0	15.2	24.4	15.6		
6	3	5	7	2	3	8	393.4	19.8	7.1	9.0	5.1	9.8	8.0	159.3	8
	21	14	13	19	21	22		12.2	11.9	11.0	15.9	16.6	20.0	60 %	
	14	10	17	18	16	10		6.0	9.9	15.5	14.7	13.6	7.2		
7	10	9	9	9	10	6	332.8	14.4	8.2	12.6	6.9	10.4	9.9	177.8	5
	23	2	10	10	21	23		18.6	4.7	6.4	15.4	23.3	17.0	47 %	
	12	20	13	15	20	15		12.0	13.8	9.7	11.7	17.3	13.8		

Table IV.4: Period by period scheduling policy; MSB procedure.

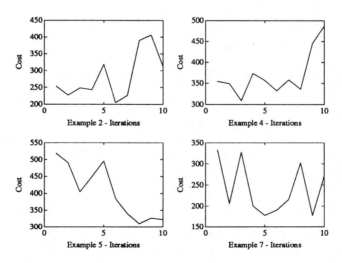

Figure IV-12: Period by period scheduling policy; MSB procedure.

Jumps of the cost may be induced by this remark. Consider iteration k of the iterative procedure, in which the optimal plan P_k (cost g_k) has been computed using sequence y_k. Even if, at each period, the schedule is determined optimally, it is still possible that the final sequence y_{k+1} is not optimal on the horizon H, and is worst than y_k.

One way to attenuate this problem is to modify the policy by taking jobs of the following periods into account, when jobs of a given period are scheduled. Again, *fictitious* arcs (or nodes) are needed in order to differentiate jobs of different periods in the MSB procedure.

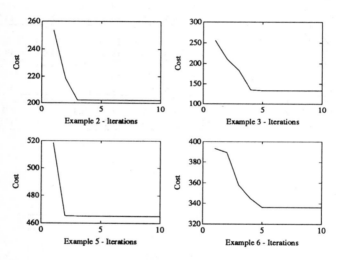

Figure IV-13: Period by period scheduling policy; MSB procedure with modification.

As in Section IV.2.1.1, to prevent jumps of the cost, we use at iteration k, y_k as the initial sequence to compute y_{k+1}, and only keep the re-optimization part in the MSB procedure. The same problems have been tested, and we only give the behavior of the procedure on some of them in Figure IV-13.

However, Remark IV.2 remains valid and, even if the cost never increases in our sample of 7 problems, other tests show that an increase of the cost is still possible.

As shown in Figure IV-14, despite the very close results obtained in Problems 2 and 3, and the smallest average computing time per iteration (12.6 seconds) obtained with the modification, the cost is often much lower without the modification. As in global scheduling, it seems interesting to let the cost oscillate.

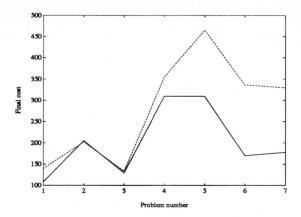

— Final cost without the modification.
- - Final cost with the modification.

Figure IV-14: Period by period scheduling policy; MSB procedure. Final costs with and without modification.

IV.2.2.2 A Priority Rule-Based Dispatching (PRD) Heuristic

The results are presented in Table IV.5. The average computing time is 17.5 seconds, approximately the same as in global scheduling. The cost improvement is still significant, even if the gain is always less than 50%.

As shown on Figure IV-15, the behavior of the procedure is very erratic. For instance, in Example 2, the cost can be very different in two successive iterations.

IV.2.2.3 Comparison between the Two Scheduling Methods

The variations of the cost are still larger when PRD is used (Figure IV-15), *i.e.*, the worst scheduling algorithm in terms of quality of the solution. However, the difference is not as clear as in global scheduling, on Figure IV-8. In Figure IV-16, looking at the final costs, the impact of the scheduling methods is still important.

Pb	Initial plan - Demands						g_i	Final plan						g_f $100(1-g_f/g_i)$	Nb iter.
1	7	7	10	3	7	9	314.0	15.1	7.6	11.4	9.6	7.0	9.0		10
	15	6	20	20	17	10		14.6	5.4	17.6	16.8	16.1	10.0	170.9	
	22	12	21	19	11	14		14.3	11.6	14.5	11.3	11.9	13.9	46 %	
2	4	6	8	7	3	9	395.7	8.5	6.0	9.8	10.9	9.3	10.6		4
	12	10	23	21	10	17		9.7	10.0	17.1	17.1	3.7	11.6	352.8	
	19	12	16	18	23	13		15.9	1.5	15.1	12.1	23.0	13.9	11 %	
3	5	3	5	2	9	9	315.7	9.9	7.7	9.3	9.8	9.0	9.7		9
	11	19	10	24	12	11		15.5	14.2	5.7	16.2	12.0	15.1	196.0	
	12	8	19	23	11	22		2.6	8.1	11.6	17.5	11.0	14.2	38 %	
4	8	4	3	7	10	3	728.4	12.4	4.0	10.0	10.2	10.0	8.9		9
	16	7	23	23	11	21		11.1	9.3	15.4	17.2	11.0	13.1	373.3	
	10	17	20	17	19	21		9.4	10.9	12.0	13.6	19.0	13.3	49 %	
5	4	8	4	5	7	5	880.6	15.4	4.9	13.0	8.1	7.0	7.8		9
	17	21	24	11	20	22		7.7	12.2	14.8	7.9	19.4	14.8	478.0	
	22	2	13	16	25	11		18.7	5.2	6.5	16.0	17.3	15.3	46 %	
6	3	5	7	2	3	8	290.8	11.9	5.0	6.7	7.5	8.8	8.0		10
	21	14	13	19	21	22		12.1	14.0	13.3	13.5	14.0	18.5	203.1	
	14	10	17	18	16	10		14.0	8.8	12.4	12.8	17.2	11.5	30 %	
7	10	9	9	9	10	6	453.6	14.4	5.7	10.4	7.7	10.1	9.1		9
	23	2	10	10	21	23		18.6	5.3	4.0	14.7	20.9	19.4	332.3	
	12	20	13	15	20	15		11.5	9.6	12.3	11.5	14.1	15.5	27 %	

Table IV.5: Period by period scheduling policy; PRD heuristic.

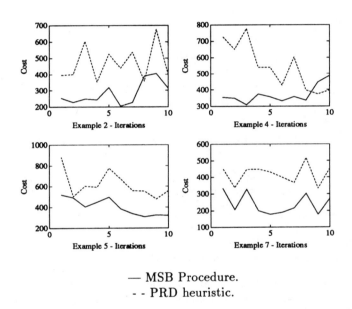

— MSB Procedure.
- - PRD heuristic.

Figure IV-15: Period by period scheduling policy; MSB procedure and PRD heuristic.

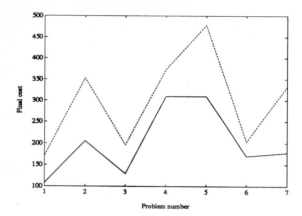

— Final cost with MSB procedure.
- - Final cost with PRD heuristic.

Figure IV-16: Period by period scheduling policy. Final costs with the two scheduling methods.

IV.2.3   Comparison between the Two Scheduling Policies

In both global and period by period policies, we showed the impact of the two scheduling methods. We now compare both policies.

In our sample, it appears that the final solution obtained by the global scheduling policy is always better than in the period by period scheduling policy (see Figure IV-17), no matter the scheduling algorithm. This difference is significant in Problems 3 and 6. Considering the average computing time per iteration, the second policy is better for MSB, but roughly the same as the first policy for PRD.

Actually, the two policies are not competing, since global scheduling is always preferable. Nevertheless, in the latter policy, because all the jobs are scheduled simultaneously, operations of jobs associated to a period may be set before (respectively after) operations of jobs of previous (respectively following) periods. Consequently, the time between the first and the last operation of a job (the processing time of the entire job, or *cycle time*) is larger than in the period by period scheduling policy.

Moreover, period by period scheduling may be imposed by technological constraints. For instance, a job may not be able to start at the time initially scheduled, because the replenishment in raw material is often made at the latest possible mo-

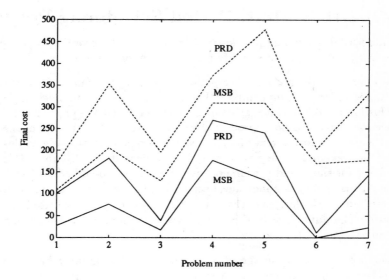

— Final cost in the global scheduling policy.
- - Final cost in the period by period scheduling policy.

Figure IV-17: Final costs with the two scheduling methods, and in the two policies.

ment. In some cases, a too long cycle time is impossible (for perishable products, for example).

Furthermore, the total amount of time that jobs are spending in Work-In-Process (WIP) inventories (*i.e.*, waiting between two resources) corresponds to the time during which the jobs are not on a resource. The WIP inventory cost is often considered negligible. But, since the time to process the jobs on the resources is fixed (equal to the sum of the processing times), increasing the cycle time of the jobs means increasing the time they spend in the WIP inventories. And the WIP inventory cost may no longer be negligible.

IV.2.4   Other Multi-Period Scheduling Policies

Other multi-period scheduling policies may be considered, according to some characteristics of the system, or to simplify the resolution of the problem.

One of the most straighforward is a period by period policy more *restrictive* than the one studied before. We may impose that a job must begin and finish in the same period. This kind of constraint may come from the fact that the products cannot be stored for a long time and no in-process inventory is allowed at the end of the week, or the WIP inventory cost is very high. Perishable products (fruits, vegetables, milk, ...) are a typical example. They must be quickly prepared and distributed, in order to be available for shops and consumers with the longest possible duration.

This particular policy is important, because it allows a total decoupling between each period. In particular, the scheduling algorithm may be executed on parallel machines. The advantage of this policy when planning on a rolling horizon is discussed in Section IV.4.

Another policy is based on the idea that if a job of a period t has to start in period $t - 1$ in an optimal schedule, it is rarely useful to start this job in a period preceding $t - 1$. A first strategy is to consider the global scheduling policy with these new constraints (precedence constraints and release dates).

A second strategy is to consider, in the scheduling problem to be solved at each iteration, only problems with the jobs of two consecutive periods t and $t + 1$. Once a problem is solved, the sequence of operations o_{ijkt} of jobs of period t is fixed as well as those preceding an operation o_{ijkt}. Then, the next problem is to schedule the operations o_{ijkt+1} not fixed, with those of jobs of period $t + 2$.

Actually, the algorithm briefly described above tries to solve the problem on a disjunctive graph, like the one in Figure IV-10, in which there is a disjunctive arc between operations of consecutive periods t and $t + 1$ that use the same machine k (o_{ijkt} and $o_{i'j'kt+1}$), but a conjunctive arc between operations o_{ijkt} and $o_{i'j'kt'}$ if $t' > t + 1$.

The advantages of this policy in the iterative procedure are mainly the decrease of the computing time, and the small increase of the final cost that one can expect. However, this policy still remains to be studied and implemented.

IV.3 Influence of the Backlogging Cost

In this short section, we want to show how the iterative procedure reacts when the backlogging costs are different from one product to another one. One checks that, by artificially increasing the backlogging cost of a product, the procedure will try to satisfy the demand for this product in each period.

We considered roblem 5 in our sample of 7 problems described in the beginning of Section IV.2, and used the MSB procedure in the global scheduling policy. By looking at the best plan obtained in Table IV.1, we observe that some demands are backlogged for products 2, 3, and 4.

Priority	Initial plan - Demands						g_i	Final plan						g_f
	4	8	4	5	7	5		4.0	8.0	8.7	5.0	7.0	10.8	
	17	21	24	11	20	22	434.3	17.0	14.8	18.4	13.2	20.0	16.2	130.8
	22	2	13	16	25	11		22.0	6.8	13.9	10.5	25.0	11.0	
Product 2								5.6	8.3	11.2	5.3	7.0	6.7	
							539.1	17.9	16.8	16.8	11.4	20.0	16.8	160.3
								19.5	5.9	13.0	12.0	25.0	14.5	
Product 3								4.5	9.7	10.6	4.9	6.8	9.6	
							434.3	19.8	14.4	17.4	11.7	19.0	17.4	100.6
								18.7	5.3	13.0	15.4	26.3	11.0	
Product 4								8.7	8.6	11.5	5.0	9.6	7.1	
							443.1	21.0	11.0	13.2	13.1	17.4	19.6	193.9
								10.2	11.0	16.3	13.9	25.0	11.3	
Product 2								4.0	10.3	5.5	5.9	3.2	9.1	
							719.9	17.0	18.7	12.8	10.1	15.0	14.4	395.0
								22.0	2.0	16.1	9.7	33.8	14.5	
Products 2 and 4								4.2	10.3	9.9	5.0	7.6	6.4	
							837.0	19.6	18.7	12.0	12.5	19.4	18.4	148.3
								16.6	2.0	16.6	14.5	25.0	13.2	

Table IV.6: Global scheduling policy; MSB procedure.

In Table IV.6, we gave the priority alternatively to each of these products. To do so, we impose that $c_{it}^- = 20$, $t = 1..3$ (backlogging cost), for the product i which has the priority, and $c_{it}^- = 10$, $t = 1..3$, for the others.

The demand becomes satisfied for products 3 and 4. However, even if the overall demand is satisfied for product 2, it is not satisfied in each period. We increased the backlogging cost for product 2: $c_{2t}^- = 100$, $t = 1..3$. Then, a *feasible* production plan is determined, for which the demand for product 2 is satisfied in each period.

Giving priority to a product means often preventing other products from having their demands satisfied. A priority ordering is established, in which the smallest backlogging costs are given to the products with the lowest priority. For instance, the last test in Table IV.6 gives the highest priority to product 1 by setting $c_{2t}^- = 100$, $t = 1..3$, then to product 4 by setting $c_{4t}^- = 20$, $t = 1..3$. Again, all the demands for these two products are satisfied, whereas some demands on product 1 and 3 are not satisfied.

In the iterative procedure, the planning level, by fixing adequate lot sizes, drives the scheduling level to find sequences such that the demands of products with high priority are satisfied. Of course, the fact that the demands can be satisfied or not depends also on the capacity of the worskshop, on the scheduling policy, and on the quality of the scheduling algorithm.

IV.4   Rolling Horizon

In the previous examples, but also in the ones which will be presented in Chapter V, the initial stock is equal to 0. Choosing an initial inventory different from 0 neither changes the method nor the validity of the conclusions that we derived. However, the problem gets more complicated when using a **rolling horizon** in which, at every beginning of the period, the production plan is re-calculated over the same number of periods (Figure IV-18).

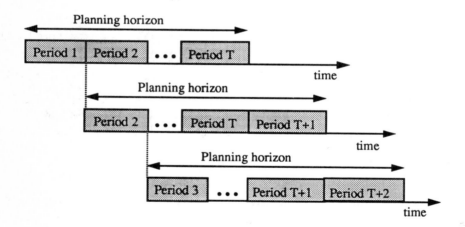

Figure IV-18: Planning on a rolling horizon.

When scheduling with the two main multi-period scheduling policies described in this chapter (global and period by period), a job J_{it} may start, and will often start, in a period preceding t. Thus, in a rolling horizon and when planning at the beginning of period t, it is no longer possible to modify the quantities $X_{it'}$ ($t' \geq t$), determined on the horizon $[t - 1, .., t + T - 2]$ and associated to jobs $J_{it'}$ in process, *i.e.*, that started before t. These quantities $X_{it'}$ correspond to in-process inventories in the workshop at the beginning of period t, and will be fixed at their current values in our model. We will only compute the size of the lots associated to jobs not in the workshop yet.

It is necessary to suppress the operations processed before period t in the constaints of the planning model, and at the scheduling level. Moreover, for each operation $o_{ijkt'}$ in-process at the beginning of period t, a release date equal to the completion time of $o_{ijkt'}$ has to be given to every operation using machine k.

Let us consider the other multi-period scheduling policies described in Section IV.2.4. In the *strict* period by period policy, using a rolling horizon does not bring any change since every job J_{it} must start and finish in period t.

If we consider the policy in which a job J_{it} cannot start before period $t - 1$, the modifications are the same than in the first two policies already discussed. In this case, we are sure that, when planning in the beginning of period t, only the quantities X_{it} may be fixed, since only jobs of period t can start in period $t - 1$ (decided in the problem of horizon $[t - 1, .., t + T - 2]$).

In Chapter V, Section V.3, we present an extension of the integrated model which is more suited to rolling horizon planning. This extension consists of taking the Work-In-Process (WIP) inventories into account in the model.

$$*$$

$$*\qquad*$$

Chapter V

Extensions of the Model

V.1 Introduction

In this chapter, we present three extensions of the integrated model developed in Chapters III and IV.

In many cases, backlogging is not allowed so that demand must always be satisfied. Thus, when the workshop capacity is limited, subcontracting some work to other companies is sometimes the only way out. The first extension we propose includes a subcontracting option with an associated cost.

The second extension considers explicitly the *Work-In-Process* (WIP) inventories between machines. In the previous model, jobs could wait between two operations but the size of the job was the same for all the operations in the routing. With this second extension, after a job has been processed on some machine, some items of the lot may wait in the WIP inventory of the next machine in the routing, and will be eventually processed later with another lot. WIP inventories are penalized in the criterion via some (WIP) holding cost coefficient. Thus, some control on the WIP inventory is possible.

Finally, in order to improve the efficiency of the procedure, we may also use a *lot-streaming* option, *i.e.,* the jobs X_{it} may be split in, for instance, s sublots X_{it}^p, $p = 1, .., s$, not necessarily of the same size. In doing so, it is easier to satisfy the capacity constraints but at the price of an increase in the size of the model.

V.2 Subcontracting

When backlogging is not permitted, and if the workshop capacity is limited, subcontracting some work to another company may be necessary.

V.2.1   Model Modifications

An easy way to model this option is to split the quantity X_{it} into a quantity X_{it}^+ produced in the workshop and a quantity X_{it}^- subcontracted outside the workshop (in another workshop or in a subcontracting company). Of course we must have:

$$X_{it} = X_{it}^+ + X_{it}^- \quad \forall i, t$$

The latest delivery date of X_{it}^- negotiated with the subcontracting company is the end of period t, and c_{it}^{st} is the per unit subcontracting cost.

Moreover, the inventory of finished products is now constrained to be positive since backlogging is not allowed any more. Therefore, it is represented by a single variable I_{it} (≥ 0).

The modified criterion is

$$\min \sum_{t=1}^{T} \sum_{i=1}^{n} (c_{it}.I_{it} + c_{it}^{pr} X_{it}^+ + c_{it}^{st}.X_{it}^-)$$

The inventory balance equation (1) in $P_{SC}(y)$ becomes

$$I_{it} - I_{it-1} - (X_{it}^+ + X_{it}^-) + D_{it} = 0 \quad i = 1,..,n; t = 1,..,T \quad (1)$$

and, of course,

$$X_{it}^+ \geq 0 \quad \forall i, t \quad (2)$$
$$X_{it}^- \geq 0 \quad \forall i, t \quad (2')$$

All the capacity constraints (5), (7), (9), and (10) are written in terms of the variables X_{it}^+ since X_{it}^- is not produced in the workshop.

The planning model with subcontracting option is now:

$$P_{SC}^{st}(y) \begin{cases} \min \sum_{t=1}^{T} \sum_{i=1}^{n} (c_{it}.I_{it} + \mathbf{c}_{it}^{st}.\mathbf{X}_{it}^-) & & \\ \mathbf{I}_{it} - \mathbf{I}_{it-1} - (\mathbf{X}_{it-1}^+ + \mathbf{X}_{it}^-) + \mathbf{D}_{it} & = 0 & i = 1,..,n; t = 1,..,T & (1) \\ \mathbf{X}_{it}^+ & \geq 0 & \forall i, t & (2) \\ \mathbf{X}_{it}^- & \geq 0 & \forall i, t & (2') \\ I_{it} & \geq 0 & \forall i, t & (3) \\ t_{ijkt} - t_{ij'k't} - p_{ij'k't}^u.\mathbf{X}_{it}^+ & \geq 0 & \forall (o_{ij'k't}, o_{ijkt}) \in A & (5) \\ t_{ijkt} & \geq 0 & \forall o_{ijkt} \in N & (6) \\ t_{ijkt} - t_{i'j'kt'} - p_{i'j'kt'}^u.\mathbf{X}_{i't'}^+ & \geq 0 & \forall (o_{i'j'kt'}, o_{ijkt}) \in S(y) & (7) \\ t_{ijkt} + p_{ijkt}^u.\mathbf{X}_{it}^+ & \leq \sum_{l=1}^{t} c_l & \forall o_{ijkt} \in L & (9) \\ t_{ijkt} + p_{ijkt}^u.\mathbf{X}_{it}^+ & \geq \sum_{l=1}^{t-1} c_l & \forall o_{ijkt} \in L & (10) \end{cases}$$

Proposition V.1
In replacing $P_{SC}(y)$ by $P_{SC}^{st}(y)$ in the ideal iterative procedure of Chapter III, Theorem III.1 is still valid.

V.2.2   Experimental Results

We have tested the iterative procedure, with P_{SC}^{st} at the planning level and the modified shifting bottleneck procedure MSB at the lower (scheduling) level. The sample consists of the same seven problems. The period-by-period and global scheduling policies have been tested, with a constant value for the subcontracting cost coefficients $c_{it}^{st} = 10$ (Table V.1).

The relative gain is always important, over 30% in 6 out of 7 problems. The procedure still anticipates some production (at the price of some holding cost) to avoid too much subcontracting.

We have also compared the optimal cost determined by this procedure with the optimal cost obtained by imposing the constraint

$$X_{it}^- + X_{it}^+ = D_{it} \quad \forall i, t.$$

in $P_{SC}^{st}(y^*)$. In this case, the total production at each period is equal to the demand (zero inventories).

The results in Table V.2 clearly show a significant gap. Of course this gap strongly depends on the subcontracting costs c_{it}^{st}.

V.3   Work-In-Process Inventories

In the model presented in Chapter III, WIP inventories are not controlled and the size of a job J_{it} is the same for all the operations in the routing. In the model below, we explicitly take WIP inventories into account. We thus allow that, after being processed on some machine k, some items of a job J_{it} stay in the WIP inventory in front of the next machine after k in the routing of J_{it}. These items are eventually processed later and possibly with some other items of a job $J_{it'}$ ($t' > t$). Some control on the WIP inventories is thus possible.

V.3.1   Model Modifications

In the example of Figure V-1 (3 jobs and 3 machines), between some operations, we have included WIP inventories with different capacities.

Some items of job J_1, after being processed on machine 1 (operation o_{111}), may wait in the WIP inventory of machine 2. Conversely, at the next period, one may increase the size of the lot of job J_{1t+1} to be processed at operation o_{122} with some of these items. The size X_{it} of the job J_{it} is not constant over the routing any more. Let us recall the formulation of the linear programming problem $P_{SC}(y)$:

Global policy; MSB procedure.

Pb	Initial Plan						Cost 1st it.	Final Plan						Cost (gain)	Nb iter.
	7	7	10	3	7	9		11.0	5.8	12.6	5.4	7.0	9.0		
1	15	6	20	20	17	10	51.3	11.0	6.0	18.1	17.1	17.0	10.0	26.2	10
	22	12	21	19	11	14		22.0	12.0	20.3	19.0	11.0	14.0	(49)	
	4	6	8	7	3	9		6.2	5.3	10.1	9.4	3.0	6.5		
2	12	10	23	21	10	17	72.6	9.8	7.1	20.9	18.6	10.0	17.0	67.9	8
	19	12	16	18	23	13		19.0	12.0	16.0	18.0	23.0	13.0	(6)	
	5	3	5	2	9	9		5.0	5.6	5.0	8.4	9.0	12.3		
3	11	19	10	24	12	11	60.7	11.0	16.1	11.4	18.7	12.0	11.3	22.7	8
	12	8	19	23	11	22		12.0	8.0	17.6	21.8	11.0	18.4	(63)	
	8	4	3	7	10	3		8.0	0.7	4.4	7.0	10.0	11.5		
4	16	7	23	23	11	21	206.4	16.0	8.4	21.5	18.5	11.0	13.4	139.1	6
	10	17	20	17	19	21		10.0	12.6	20.0	17.0	19.0	18.3	(33)	
	4	8	4	5	7	5		4.0	7.3	11.6	5.1	7.0	9.3		
5	17	21	24	11	20	22	205.0	17.9	14.7	16.4	10.9	20.0	17.7	82.6	8
	22	2	13	16	25	11		21.1	2.0	13.0	16.0	25.0	11.0	(60)	
	3	5	7	2	3	8		3.0	5.0	7.2	2.3	3.0	8.0		
6	21	14	13	19	21	22	20.6	21.0	14.0	12.2	18.7	21.0	22.0	0.5	10
	14	10	17	18	16	10		14.0	10.0	17.0	18.0	16.0	10.0	(98)	
	10	9	9	9	10	6		10.1	8.3	11.2	10.0	10.0	7.6		
7	23	2	10	10	21	23	227.0	22.9	6.3	7.8	7.3	21.0	21.4	37.3	9
	12	20	13	15	20	15		12.0	15.3	13.0	15.0	20.0	15.0	(84)	

Period by period policy; MSB procedure.

Pb	Initial Plan						Cost 1st it.	Final Plan						Cost (gain)	Nb iter.
	7	7	10	3	7	9		9.0	5.8	10.0	9.8	7.0	6.7		
1	15	6	20	20	17	10	139.2	19.4	5.5	15.8	16.3	17.0	11.6	110.9	10
	22	12	21	19	11	14		15.6	12.0	21.0	15.0	11.0	12.4	(20)	
	4	6	8	7	3	9		10.2	4.5	6.9	9.5	6.0	8.2		
2	12	10	23	21	10	17	190.4	17.5	12.2	17.6	18.5	9.0	14.1	144.6	9
	19	12	16	18	23	13		7.2	9.8	16.0	18.0	21.0	13.0	(24)	
	5	3	5	2	9	9		5.8	3.3	6.4	11.1	9.0	9.6		
3	11	19	10	24	12	11	197.4	19.9	12.7	13.2	15.7	14.4	13.9	101.5	7
	12	8	19	23	11	22		2.4	8.0	14.4	22.2	8.6	17.7	(49)	
	8	4	3	7	10	3		12.2	4.0	6.7	6.7	10.0	8.6		
4	16	7	23	23	11	21	301.4	14.9	9.4	15.6	16.3	11.0	13.2	238.8	9
	10	17	20	17	19	21		6.9	12.0	19.3	17.0	19.0	15.4	(21)	
	4	8	4	5	7	5		10.0	8.7	12.2	5.9	9.8	7.5		
5	17	21	24	11	20	22	264.7	18.6	12.0	14.5	12.7	17.2	12.3	199.3	9
	22	2	13	16	25	11		14.4	2.0	13.0	13.4	25.0	11.0	(25)	
	3	5	7	2	3	8		6.3	4.3	2.2	5.3	6.0	6.0		
6	21	14	13	19	21	22	233.6	24.1	12.5	13.0	15.7	18.0	22.0	104.7	3
	14	10	17	18	16	10		7.6	10.0	17.0	18.0	16.0	10.0	(55)	
	10	9	9	9	10	6		14.6	8.8	7.9	7.5	10.9	6.0		
7	23	2	10	10	21	23	293.8	18.4	7.0	13.7	15.0	21.9	13.4	146.2	3
	12	20	13	15	20	15		12.0	15.0	9.3	10.0	18.1	15.0	(50)	

( ) : Relative gain in %.

Table V.1: Subcontracting option. $c_{it}^{st} = 10, \quad \forall i, t.$

Problem		1	2	3	4	5	6	7
global	final cost	26.3	67.9	22.7	139.1	82.6	0.5	37.3
	cost for $X = D$	59.4	83.3	105.4	211.1	157.5	3.1	67.9
period by	final cost	110.9	144.6	101.5	238.8	199.3	104.7	146.2
period	cost for $X = D$	191.7	206.3	259.5	313.1	306.9	138.9	219.9

Table V.2: Subcontracting option. $c_{it}^{st} = 10 \quad \forall i, t$.

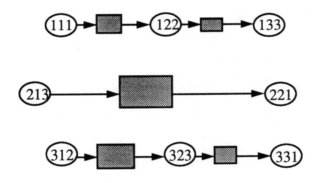

◼ : Work-In-Process inventories between operations.

Figure V-1: WIP inventories.

$$P_{SC}(y) \begin{cases} \min \sum_{t=1}^{T} \sum_{i=1}^{n} (c_{it}^{+}.I_{it}^{+} + c_{it}^{-}.I_{it}^{-}) \\ (I_{it}^{+} - I_{it}^{-}) - (I_{it-1}^{+} - I_{it-1}^{-}) - X_{it} + D_{it} & = 0 & i = 1,..,n; t = 1,..,T & (1) \\ X_{it} & \geq 0 & \forall i, t & (2) \\ I_{it}^{+} & \geq 0 & \forall i, t & (3) \\ I_{it}^{-} & \geq 0 & \forall i, t & (4) \\ t_{ijkt} - t_{ij'k't} - p_{ij'k't}^{u}.X_{it} & \geq 0 & \forall(o_{ij'k't}, o_{ijkt}) \in A & (5) \\ t_{ijkt} & \geq 0 & \forall o_{ijkt} \in N & (6) \\ t_{ijkt} - t_{i'j'kt'} - p_{i'j'kt'}^{u}.X_{i't'} & \geq 0 & \forall(o_{i'j'kt'}, o_{ijkt}) \in S(y) & (7) \\ t_{ijkt} + p_{ijkt}^{u}.X_{it} & \leq \sum_{l=1}^{t} c_l & \forall o_{ijkt} \in L & (9) \\ t_{ijkt} + p_{ijkt}^{u}.X_{it} & \geq \sum_{l=1}^{t-1} c_l & \forall o_{ijkt} \in L & (10) \end{cases}$$

Let X_{ijkt} be the quantity to be processed at operation o_{ijkt} in the routing of the job J_{it}. For the last operations in the routing, we have:

Remark V.1

For the last operations $o_{ijkt} \in L$, $X_{ijkt} = X_{it}$, where X_{it} is the quantity to be completed by the end of period t.

Of course, we also have

$$X_{ijkt} \geq 0 \quad \forall o_{ijkt} \in N \quad (2')$$

Constraints (5) and (7) are modified as follows:

$$t_{ijkt} - t_{ij'k't} - p_{ij'k't}^{u}.\mathbf{X_{ij'k't}} \geq 0 \quad \forall(o_{ij'k't}, o_{ijkt}) \in A \quad (5)$$

$$t_{ijkt} - t_{i'j'kt'} - p_{i'j'kt'}^{u}.\mathbf{X_{i'j'kt'}} \geq 0 \quad \forall(o_{i'j'kt'}, o_{ijkt}) \in S \quad (7)$$

Following Remark V.1:

$$X_{ijkt} - X_{it} = 0 \quad \forall o_{ijkt} \in L \quad (11)$$

Thus Constraints (9) and (10) are not modified.

Let Q_{ijkt} be the WIP inventory between operation $o_{ijkt} \notin L$ and its successor, and let F be the set of first operations for all the jobs.

If $o_{ij'k't}$ is the operation preceding $o_{ijkt} \notin F$ then necessarily:

$$X_{ijkt} \leq X_{ij'k't} + Q_{ij'k't-1}$$

and we have the WIP inventory balance equation

$$Q_{ij'k't} - Q_{jk't-1} - (X_{ij'k't} - X_{ijkt}) = 0 \quad \forall(o_{ij'k't}, o_{ijkt}) \in A \quad (12)$$
$$Q_{ijkt} \geq 0 \quad \forall o_{ijkt} \in N, \ o_{ijkt} \notin L \quad (13)$$

Let c_{ijkt}^{int} be the per unit WIP holding cost associated to Q_{ijkt}. The criterion is now:

$$\min \sum_{t=1}^{T} \sum_{i=1}^{n} (c_{it}^{+}.I_{it}^{+} + c_{it}^{-}.I_{it}^{-} + \sum_{o_{ijkt}\in N_{it},\, o_{ijkt}\notin L} (c_{ijkt}^{int}.Q_{ijkt}))$$

where N_{it} is the set of operations in the routing of job J_{it}.

To simplify, we impose that $c_{ijkt}^{int} = c_{it}^{int}$ for all $(ijkt)$, so that we only need to consider the total WIP inventory of job J_{it}, i.e., $Q_{it} = \sum_{o_{ijkt}\in N_{it},\, o_{ijkt}\notin L} Q_{ijkt}$. The criterion becomes

$$\min \sum_{t=1}^{T} \sum_{i=1}^{n} (c_{it}^{+}.I_{it}^{+} + c_{it}^{-}.I_{it}^{-} + c_{it}^{int}.Q_{it})$$

We also have the relationship

$$Q_{it} - Q_{it-1} - (X_{ijkt} - X_{it}) = 0, \quad \forall j,t;\ o_{ijkt} \in F. \quad (14)$$

We may further simplify and replace (12) and (13) by

$$Q_{ij'k'0} + \sum_{l=1}^{t} (X_{ij'k'l} - X_{ijkl}) \geq 0, \quad \forall (o_{ij'k't}, o_{ijkt}) \in A \quad (15)$$

so that we finally get the following planning problem with WIP inventories:

$$P_{SC}^{int}(y) \begin{cases} \min \sum_{t=1}^{T} \sum_{i=1}^{n} (c_{it}^{+}.I_{it}^{+} + c_{it}^{-}.I_{it}^{-} + c_{it}^{int}.Q_{it}) & & \\ (I_{it}^{+} - I_{it}^{-}) - (I_{it-1}^{+} - I_{it-1}^{-}) - X_{it} + D_{it} &= 0 & i=1,..,n; t=1,..,T & (1) \\ X_{it} &\geq 0 & \forall i,t & (2) \\ X_{ijkt} &\geq 0 & \forall o_{ijkt} \in \mathbf{N} & (2') \\ I_{it}^{+} &\geq 0 & \forall i,t & (3) \\ I_{it}^{-} &\geq 0 & \forall i,t & (4) \\ t_{ijkt} - t_{ij'k't} - p_{ij'k't}^{u}.X_{ij'k't} &\geq 0 & \forall (o_{ij'k't}, o_{ijkt}) \in A & (5) \\ t_{ijkt} &\geq 0 & \forall o_{ijkt} \in \mathbf{N} & (6) \\ t_{ijkt} - t_{i'j'kt} - p_{i'j'kt'}^{u}.X_{i'j'kt'} &\geq 0 & \forall (o_{i'j'kt'}, o_{ijkt}) \in S(y) & (7) \\ t_{ijkt} + p_{ijkt}^{u}.X_{it} &\leq \sum_{l=1}^{t} c_l & \forall o_{ijkt} \in L & (9) \\ t_{ijkt} + p_{ijkt}^{u}.X_{it} &\geq \sum_{l=1}^{t-1} c_l & \forall o_{ijkt} \in L & (10) \\ X_{ijkt} - X_{it} &= 0 & \forall o_{ijkt} \in \mathbf{L} & (11) \\ Q_{it} - Q_{it-1} - (X_{ijkt} - X_{it}) &= 0 & \forall i,t;\ o_{ijkt} \in \mathbf{F} & (14) \\ Q_{ij'k'0} + \sum_{l=1}^{t} (X_{ij'k'l} - X_{ijkl}) &\geq 0 & \forall (o_{ij'k't}, o_{ijkt}) \in \mathbf{A} & (15) \end{cases}$$

Proposition V.2
In replacing $P_{SC}(y)$ by $P_{SC}^{int}(y)$ in the ideal iterative procedure in Chapter III), Theorem III.1 still holds.

Proposition V.3

For a given sequence y, the optimal values g^*_{int} and g^* of $P^{int}_{SC}(y)$ and $P_{SC}(y)$ respectively, satisfy $\mathbf{g^*_{int} \leq g^*}$.

At the scheduling level, the problem (O_1) (section III.3.2) is now:

$$
O_{int} \begin{cases}
t_{ijkt} - t_{ij'k't} - p^u_{ij'k't} \cdot \mathbf{X_{ij'k't}} & \geq 0 & \forall(o_{ij'k't}, o_{ijkt}) \in A & (1) \\[4pt]
t_{ijkt} & \geq 0 & \forall o_{ijkt} \in N & (2) \\[4pt]
\begin{cases} t_{ijkt} - t_{i'j'kt'} - p^u_{i'j'kt'} \cdot \mathbf{X_{i'j'kt'}} \geq 0 \\ \text{or} \\ t_{i'j'kt'} - t_{ijkt} - p^u_{ijkt} \cdot \mathbf{X_{ijkt}} \geq 0 \end{cases} & & \forall(o_{i'j'kt'}, o_{ijkt}) \in E_k, \ k \in M & (3) \\[4pt]
t_{ijkt} + p^u_{ijkt} \cdot \mathbf{X_{ijkt}} & \leq \displaystyle\sum_{l=1}^{t} c_l & \forall o_{ijkt} \in L & (4)
\end{cases}
$$

To be coherent with the planning level, some precedence constraints are necessary in order to ensure that the WIP inventory level $Q_{ij'k't-1}$ is available to process operation o_{ijkt} $((o_{ij'k't}, o_{ijkt}) \in A)$. Actually, it is enough to ensure that operation o_{ijkt} cannot start if $o_{ij'k't-1}$ is not completed. When using the period by period scheduling policy, those precedence constraints are always satisfied.

The number of variables in $P^{int}_{SC}(y)$ increases with the number of operations. To reduce the size of the problem, one may only consider certain WIP inventories in front of some (more important) machines. Thus, there is only one variable X_{ijkt} for all the operations between two WIP inventories.

V.3.2 Experimental Results

Again, the iterative procedure, now with $P^{int}_{SC}(y)$, has been tested on the same (seven problems) sample.

Problem		1	2	3	4	5	6	7
global	final cost with $P^{int}_{SC}(y)$	8.1	74.1	22.3	121.6	94.4	0.0	38.8
	final cost with $P_{SC}(y)$	27.9	75.7	17.6	177.2	130.8	0.3	23.1
period by	final cost with $P^{int}_{SC}(y)$	105.9	178.7	27.2	303.3	290.6	60.8	130.1
period	final cost with $P_{SC}(y)$	108.1	205.4	129.3	309.4	309.3	159.3	177.8

Table V.3: WIP inventories. $c^{int}_{it} = 0.01 \ \forall i, t$.

We first consider negligible holding WIP inventory costs by setting $c^{int}_{it} = 0.01, \ \forall i, t$ (Table V.3), and compare the results without WIP inventories.

In the period by period policy, the results are always better with WIP inventories and the gap is sometimes large. This is not true with the global policy (see Problems 3 and 6). In view of Proposition V.3, this is due the to scheduling heuristic procedure which is less efficient since it is penalized by the extra precedence constraints.

Problem		1	2	3	4	5	6	7
global	final cost with $P_{SC}^{int}(y)$	**38.1**	80.8	**9.7**	**134.8**	154.8	1.7	38.7
	final cost with $P_{SC}(y)$	**27.9**	**75.7**	17.6	177.2	**130.8**	**0.3**	**23.1**
period by	final cost with $P_{SC}^{int}(y)$	117.4	212.3	**103.6**	254.1	287.0	98.6	149.0
period	final cost with $P_{SC}(y)$	**108.1**	**205.4**	129.3	309.4	309.3	159.3	177.8

Table V.4: WIP Inventories. $c_{it}^{int} = 1.0 \ \forall i, t$.

When considering the WIP inventory costs equal to the corresponding end-product holding costs, *i.e.*, $c_{it}^{int} = 1.0$, $\forall i, t$, one gets the results in Table V.4.

In period by period, the results are even better whereas in global scheduling, the results are disappointing since the iterative procedure is more efficient without WIP inventories.

In period by period scheduling, the WIP inventories are not negligible whereas they are very small in global scheduling. To use the flexibility introduced by WIP inventories, the procedure tries to take advantage of the margins of operations in the sequence y computed at the scheduling level. And the margins are more important with the period by period policy (see for example figure IV-11) than with the global policy (see for example figure IV-2). Indeed, using the latter policy, one already exploits those margins of operations at period t to place some operations of later periods.

Another variant of the model consists in relaxing the capacity constraint (9) in $P_{SC}(y)$. Namely, the right-hand-side is now $T_{it} + \sum_{l=1}^{t} c_{lt}$ and T_{it} is penalized in the criterion with some coefficient. For more details the readeris referred to [Dauzere-Peres 92].

V.4 Lot Streaming Option

In the initial model developed in Chapters III and IV, the lot corresponding to job X_{it} cannot be split into several sublots. If we now use this option, some flexibility is provided at the scheduling level and the capacity constraints are, in principle, easier to satisfy. The price to pay is an increase of the size of the problem, which is not a major problem for the linear programming problem $P_{SC}(y)$, whereas it is a serious one for the scheduling problem, harder to solve.

V.4.1   Model Modifications

Assume that we have the option of splitting the lot of job X_{it} into, for instance, s sublots where s is a fixed integer. Let X_{it}^p, $p = 1, ..s$, be the quantity of product i in sublot p to be delivered by the end of period t. Let o_{ijkt}^p be the corresponding operations in the routing of job J_{it}.

Thus, in $P_{SC}(y)$ in Chapter III, we must include the constraint

$$\sum_{p=1}^{s} X_{it}^p = X_{it}, \quad \forall i, t.$$

Constraints (5)-(10) in $P_{SC}(y)$ are virtually the same, with now o_{ijkt}^p in place of o_{ijkt}, and X_{it}^p in place of X_{it}. Of course, the sets A, N and L in (5)-(6) and (9)-(10), as well as y, refer now to a larger graph since the number of operations has increased.

As suggested by the results presented in Chapter VI for a standard lot streaming problem, the number s need not be large. $s = 2$ might be a good compromise between efficiency and increase in the size of the problem. This option has not been tested yet.

V.5   Conclusion

The previous modifications have been tested on a limited sample of academic examples. However, they show that the initial model is not rigid and can incorporate various specifications.

More important, is is worth noting that the model may handle more sophisticated workshops than the standard job-shop. For instance, it is very easy to incorporate the fact that a machine is idle during certain intervals in certain periods. Workshops with pools of machines can also be handled.

Indeed, as soon as, at the lower level, one has a scheduling procedure able to compute a sequence y of operations on the machines, the iterative procedure described in Chapter III can be easily adapted. However, the quality of the final plan will depend on the quality of the heuristic used at the scheduling level.

*

*   *

Chapter VI

Lot Streaming

VI.1 Introduction

In this chapter, we consider an integrated model for *Lot Streaming* in a standard job-shop scheduling problem where n jobs have to be scheduled on m machines, and each machine can process only one job at a time.

A **job** is actually a **lot**, *i.e.*, composed of several items. In classical approaches, an item is processed on a machine only when the entire lot has been processed on the upstream machine. Thus, in case of large lots, items already processed on a machine wait on this machine whereas the downstream machine may be idle. This restrictive assumption may come from management considerations but in many cases, splitting a lot is possible since its size is already the outcome of a higher level lotsizing procedure. Assuming that it is possible to divide a lot into several **sublots**, a sublot can be processed on a machine even if the other sublots have not yet been processed on the upstream machine. This process is called **Lot Streaming**. The problem is to split lots into sublots in order to improve some criterion (makespan, mean flow time, weighted sum of completion times, ...), *i.e.*, to determine not only the sublot sizes, but also the sequencing of the sublots on the machines. One is interested in the following issues:

> *i) How much is it possible to improve the criterion by dividing each lot into several sublots?*
>
> *ii) How many sublots are required to achieve this improvement?*

Note that lot streaming is different from preemption. In the latter, the processing of a job on a machine can be interrupted to process a more urgent job, but the entire lot must be completed before starting processing on the next machine.

If there is no set-up time, then it is always optimal to consider the maximum number of sublots. However, the optimal makespan is much harder to compute. Moreover, on a practical standpoint, too many sublots might not be reasonable. In case of set-up times, there is a trade-off between the time saved by dividing into sublots and the extra-time due to additional set-ups. [Karmarkar 87] shows the great importance of lotsizing on time performances such as makespan and flow time.

With few exceptions, research in lotsizing and scheduling are two separate worlds. As already noted in Chapter I, and quoted from [Potts and Van Wassenhove 92] *".. both worlds seem to be very much apart. The scheduling literature nearly always assume that batching and lotsizing decisions are already taken. Similarly, research on batching and lotsizing seldom considers sequencing issues."* Lot Streaming, and in particular, the integrated model with the procedure to be presented later, try to bridge the gap.

[Szendrovits 75] solves the one-job problem with a constant and continuous demand on an infinite horizon, when the objective is to minimize the work-in-process and finished product inventories. Based on this work, [Goyal 76] stresses that the number of sublots per lot is a discrete variable, and proposes a new formulation of the cost function where a fixed cost of moving a sublot through all the machines is taken into account. Finally, [Szendrovits 76] discusses the validity of the transportation costs, and presents an improved procedure when they are considered. The lot-streaming problem for one job is also analyzed in [Triesch 87] and [Baker 87].

[Potts and Baker 89] give conditions such that *consistent* sublots (*i.e.*, for a given job, the size of the sublots is the same on each machine) are sufficient in the one-job case, and analyze the two-machine problem with and without equal sublots. Finally, the flow-shop problem with multiple jobs is studied, and a simple numerical example shows that this problem cannot be solved by first constructing an optimal sequence, and then splitting each job into optimal sublots. In fact, in the one-job case, all the sublots of a given product are produced in sequence whereas for multiple jobs, as shown by the example in [Potts and Baker 89], the optimal sequence can be such that the sublots are sequenced independently, especially when there is no set-up time.

[Baker and Pyke 90] propose an efficient algorithm for one job and two sublots. Although the problem is also solvable by Linear Programming, various simple heuristics are presented for the s-sublot case. Significant results on their 30 problem sample are given. [Kropp and Smunt 90] consider also the one-job case, and present a Linear Programming formulation when the makespan is minimized, and a Quadratic Programming formulation when the mean flow time is minimized. Two heuristics are proposed, and conclusions are derived from numerical examples.

In this chapter, we present an integrated model, along with an efficient solving procedure, for the general job-shop scheduling problem, and with the *makespan* criterion. In the one-job case, no sequencing has to be made on the machines since all the sublots are processed consequently whereas here, with multiple jobs, sublots have to be sequenced. Actually, as already mentionned, the problem is to compute **simultaneously** sublot sizes and sequences of sublots on the machines.

For a **fixed** number of sublots, the iterative procedure alternates between

- solving a **Lot-Streaming** problem for a **fixed sequence** of the sublots on the machines, and

- solving a **Job-Shop Scheduling** problem for fixed sublot sizes.

This procedure is very similar in spirit to the procedure described in Chapter III for planning and scheduling.

In the Lot-Streaming procedure (LS), given a fixed number of sublots and a sequencing of these sublots on the machine, their **optimal sizes** are determined by solving a linear programming problem which minimizes the makespan.

In the Scheduling procedure, given the fixed sizes of the sublots, a **sequencing** of the sublots on the machines is determined by minimizing the makespan in a classical job-shop scheduling problem where the sublots are processed independently.

Convergence of the procedure is analyzed and experimental results on a sample of 120 problems show that, despite its simplicity, the procedure is very efficient. Indeed:

- In the absence of set-up time, the makespan converges to a value very close to the lower bound obtained by considering the machines in "parallel". Therefore, it suggests that the procedure converges to a **global** optimum.

- More surprisingly, in all the cases, very few sublots (2 to 4) are needed (and this, independently of the size of the job).

Since the sublot sizes are real-valued, a simple rounding procedure is applied. As one may expect, its influence is negligible for large jobs but, more surprisingly, it is still not very important for small jobs.

Moreover, the improvement on the makespan after the first 2 iterations of the procedure is very small.

Finally, an important consequence of this result for standard lotsizing models is discussed.

VI.2   A Lot-Streaming Procedure

VI.2.1   Notation and Definitions

We modify the notation introduced in Chapter II, and adapted in Chapter III (Section III.2.1), to represent the sublots:

J_i : job associated to the product i
$J = [J_1, .., J_n]$: set of n jobs
$M = [1, .., m]$: set of m machines

s : (given) number of sublots per job

D_i : number of units of product i in job J_i

J_{il} : l^{th} sublot of job J_i

X_{il} : quantity of product i in sublot J_{il}

o_{ijkl} : j^{th} operation on the routing of sublot J_{il} to be processed on machine k

N : set of operations

A : set of pairs of operations constrained by precedence relations

E_k : set of pairs of operations to be performed on machine k, $E = \bigcup\limits_{k=1}^{m} E_k$

p_{ijk}^u : processing time of operations o_{ijkl} ($\forall l$) per unit of product i.

p_{ijkl} : processing time of operation o_{ijkl}

t_{ijkl} : start time of operation o_{ijkl}

L : set of last operations of the sublots

The scheduling problem can be represented using a disjunctive graph, where N is the set of nodes, A is the set of conjunctive arcs, and E the set of disjunctive arcs (see Chapter II, Section II.2.1 for details). o_{ijkl} is in L if there is no operation $o_{ij'k'l}$ such that $(o_{ijkl}, o_{ij'k'l}) \in A$.

Recall also from Chapter II, that determining a sequence y of sublots on the machines means determining a complete acyclic selection S in E, i.e., a choice of a direction for each disjunctive arc such that the directed graph $G_S = (N, A, S)$ contains no cycle.

VI.2.2 An Integrated Model

The model to be presented below is an *integrated* model since it considers *simultaneously* lotsizing and scheduling issues.

For a given number of sublots s, solving the lot-streaming problem optimally is equivalent to solving the following problem (up to the rounding procedure).

$$
LS \begin{cases}
\min\ C_{max} & & (0) \\[4pt]
\sum\limits_{l=1}^{s} X_{il} - D_i = 0 & i = 1, .., n & (1) \\[4pt]
X_{il} \geq 0 & \forall i, l & (2) \\[4pt]
t_{ijkl} - t_{ij'k'l} - p_{ij'k'}^u . X_{il} \geq 0 & \forall (o_{ij'k'l}, o_{ijkl}) \in A & (3) \\[4pt]
t_{ijkl} \geq 0 & \forall o_{ijkl} \in N & (4) \\[4pt]
\begin{cases} t_{ijkl} - t_{i'j'kl'} - p_{i'j'k}^u . X_{i'l'} \geq 0 \\ \text{or} \\ t_{i'j'kl'} - t_{ijkl} - p_{ijk}^u . X_{il} \geq 0 \end{cases} & \forall (o_{i'j'kl'}, o_{ijkl}) \in E_k,\ k \in M & (5) \\[4pt]
t_{ijkl} + p_{ijk}^u . X_{il} - C_{max} \leq 0 & (i, j, k, l)\ \ s.t.\ o_{ijkl} \in L & (6)
\end{cases}
$$

Conditions (1) ensure that all the products are made. Conditions (3) represents the conjunctive constraints on the routings, whereas conditions (5) represent the disjunctive constraints on the machines. Conditions (2) and (4) are the non-negativity conditions. The makespan (C_{max}) is determined by conditions (6). Note that in an optimal solution, even if there are s sublots, some of them may be empty, which means that less than s sublots were necessary to improve the makespan.

Actually, LS can be solved for very small instances only. Hence, we propose a two-level model and a procedure, in the spirit of the one presented in Chapter III for planning and scheduling. At the upper level (also called *lot-streaming* level), one has to solve LS where the sequencing is fixed (a selection S is given), *i.e.*, the problem $LS(S)$ where conditions (5) are replaced by:

$$t_{ijkl} - t_{i'j'kl'} - p^u_{i'j'k}.X_{i'l'} \geq 0 \qquad \forall(o_{i'j'kl'}, o_{ijkl}) \in S \qquad (5')$$

Very large instances of $LS(S)$ can be solved with any Linear Programming package.

At the lower level (or *scheduling* level), for given sublot-sizes X_{il}, sublots have to be sequenced, *i.e.*, the following standard job-shop scheduling problem has to be solved:

$$O \begin{cases} \min C_{max} & (7) \\ t_{ijkl} - t_{ij'k'l} - p_{ij'k'l} \geq 0 & \forall(o_{ij'k'l}, o_{ijkl}) \in A & (8) \\ t_{ijkl} \geq 0 & \forall o_{ijkl} \in N & (9) \\ \begin{cases} t_{ijkl} - t_{i'j'kl'} - p_{i'j'kl'} \geq 0 \\ \text{or} \\ t_{i'j'kl'} - t_{ijkl} - p_{ijkl} \geq 0 \end{cases} & \forall(o_{i'j'kl'}, o_{ijkl}) \in E_k, \ k \in M & (10) \\ t_{ijkl} + p_{ijkl} - C_{max} \leq 0 & (i,j,k,l) \ s.t. \ o_{ijkl} \in L & (11) \end{cases}$$

where $p_{ijkl} = p^u_{ijk}.X_{il}$.

This problem is still $\mathcal{NP}$-hard, but easier to solve than LS, since the sublot-sizes are fixed, and an extensive literature has been devoted to this problem (see Chapter II).

VI.2.3 An Iterative Procedure

In this section, an ideal iterative procedure for solving the model presented above is proposed. It very similar in spirit to the ideal procedure described in Chapter III for finding a feasible plan.

Step 1. Initialization. $k := 1$, $C^0_{max} := +\infty$ and $list := \emptyset$. An initial selection S_1 is fixed.

Step 2. Lot-streaming problem. Solve $LS(S_k) \rightarrow C^k_{max}$.
If $C^k_{max} < C^{k-1}_{max}$ then $list := S_k$.
If $C^k_{max} = C^{k-1}_{max}$ then $list := list \bigcup S_k$.

Step 3. Scheduling problem. Search for a selection $S \notin list$ that minimizes the makespan in problem O

If $C_{max}(S) > C_{max}^k$ then **STOP**.

Otherwise, set $k := k + 1$, $S_k := S$ and go to 1.

In Step 2, optimal sublot-sizes are determined for a fixed sequence (selection S_k). In Step 3, the goal is to find a better sequence not in $list$ for these sublots. If this sequence does not exist, one stops. $list$ is introduced to avoid cycles. Obviously, the sequence of makespans C_{max}^k is monotone non-increasing and converges in a finite number of steps to a value denoted C_{max}^*. Actually, the following theorem is proved.

Theorem VI.1 *The ideal iterative procedure stops after a finite number of iterations with a final sequence (selection S^*), sublot-sizes X_{il}^*, and makespan C_{max}^*. Moreover, C_{max}^* (and the associated sublot-sizes) is a locally optimal solution of the global problem LS.*

Proof:

First, we prove that the procedure stops after a finite number of iterations. Let Y be the set of all the admissible selections S (or sequences). An optimal makespan $C_{max}(S)$ is associated to each selection S in Y by solving $LS(S)$. Since, by construction of the procedure, a selection cannot be picked out more than once, and because Y is a finite set, the procedure stops after a finite number of iterations with a selection S^*, and an associated makespan C_{max}^*. Actually, C_{max}^* is the minimum makespan among the subset Y' of selections in Y ($Y' \subseteq Y$) that have been chosen in the procedure: $C_{max}^* = \min_{S \in Y'} C_{max}(S)$.

Now, we prove that the solution is locally optimal. If not, then there is an infinite sequence of sublot-sizes and sequences (X_{il}^k, S^k) converging to (X_{il}^*, S^*), and such that $C_{max}^k < C_{max}^*$, where C_{max}^k is computed with X_{il}^k. Since Y is finite, there is a subsequence $(X_{il}^{k'}, S^{k'})$ such that $S^{k'} = S'$, $\forall k'$. All the start times of this subsequence are in the interval $[0, C_{max}^*]$ (otherwise, $C_{max}^{k'}$ would be greater than C_{max}^*) which is a compact set. Therefore, there exists another subsequence $(X_{il}^{k''}, S')$ where $t_{ijkl}^{k''}$ converges to some $t_{ijkl}'' \in [0, C_{max}^*]$ for every operation o_{ijkl}.

Now, since $X_{il}^{k''}$ and $t_{ijkl}^{k''}$ both converge, by continuity, in $LS(S')$, the constraints (3), (5'), and (6) satisfied by $(X_{il}^{k''}, t_{ijkl}^{k''})$ are also satisfied by (X_{il}^*, t_{ijkl}''). Therefore, the sublot-sizes X_{il}^* are feasible for the selection S' and, in Step 3 of the procedure, S' would have been selected and would have yield a makespan strictly lower than C_{max}^* in Step 2 of the next iteration, a contradiction. ♣

However, getting an optimal solution to the scheduling problem in Step 3 is almost impossible for realistic size problems, so that, for practical purposes, Step 3 is replaced by:

3. **Scheduling problem.** Search for S which minimizes the makespan with some given *heuristic method*.

   Set $k := k + 1$, $S_k := S$ and go to 2.

The procedure stops if the makespan remains constant for 2 iterations, or after a finite number of iterations. In the implemented algorithm, in contrast to the ideal procedure, a monotone decrease of the makespan is not guaranteed any more, since a heuristic method may find a selection S in Step 3 with a makespan worse than $C_{max}(S_k)$.

VI.2.4 The Rounding Procedure

The above algorithm stops with real-valued sublots. However, in principle, only integer-valued sublots make sense. Therefore we also propose a simple rounding procedure. For each product i, if there are s positive sublots, then all the sublots X_{il}, $l = 1, .., s - 1$, are rounded to the closest integer and the last sublot X_{is} is $D_i - \sum_{l=1}^{s-1} X_{il}$. Then, the new makespan is calculated with the integer-valued sublots. If D_i is large enough, this rounding is expected to have a small effect on the makespan.

VI.2.5 The Model with Set-Up Times

Set-up times τ_{ijk} are easy to consider in our model by introducing a Boolean variable y_{il} for each X_{il}. y_{il} is equal to zero when $X_{il} = 0$, and equal to 1 when $X_{il} > 0$. In the following formulation, the coupling between set-up and production variables is ensured by constraints (19).

$$
LS_{set}(S) \begin{cases}
\min\ C_{max} & & & (12) \\
\sum_{l=1}^{s} X_{il} - D_i & = 0 & i = 1, .., n & (13) \\
X_{il} & \geq 0 & \forall i, l & (14) \\
t_{ijkl} - t_{ij'k'l} - p_{ij'k'}^u . X_{il} - \tau_{ij'k'} . y_{il} & \geq 0 & \forall (o_{ij'k'l}, o_{ijkl}) \in A & (15) \\
t_{ijkl} & \geq 0 & \forall o_{ijkl} \in N & (16) \\
t_{ijkl} - t_{i'j'kl'} - p_{i'j'k}^u . X_{i'l'} - \tau_{i'j'k} . y_{i'l'} & \geq 0 & \forall (o_{i'j'kl'}, o_{ijkl}) \in S & (17) \\
t_{ijkl} + p_{ijk}^u . X_{il} + \tau_{ijk} . y_{il} - C_{max} & \leq 0 & (i, j, k, l)\ s.t.\ o_{ijkl} \in L & (18) \\
D_i . y_{il} - X_{il} & \geq 0 & i = 1, .., n; l = 1, .., s & (19) \\
y_{il} & \in \{0, 1\} & \forall i, l & (20)
\end{cases}
$$

The theorem is still valid when $LS_{set}(S)$ is solved in Step 2 of the *ideal* iterative procedure. However, the proof is more delicate. Because of eventual zero components of X^*, the continuity argument cannot be invoked any more.

With these Boolean variables, our problem becomes a Mixed-Integer Linear Programming problem, and therefore cannot be solved as easily as $LS(S)$. However, the problem can be simplified by imposing that a given number of sublots are always non-empty, *i.e.*, by setting to 1 the Boolean variables associated to these sublots. Actually, an easier solution will be to transform $LS_{set}(S)$ into a Linear Programming problem by forcing all the sublots to be non-empty. In this case, the makespan will increase with the number of sublots s after a given threshold on s.

Another natural improvement would be to omit the set-up time, in constraint (17), when two sublots of a same product are sequenced consecutively on a machine. This modification is not included in our numerical experiments since the scheduling algorithm, used in Step 3 of the procedure, does not take this into account.

VI.2.6   A Lower Bound

A lower bound on the optimal makespan is given by:

$$LB = \max_{k \in M}(\sum_{J_i \in J^k} p_{ijk}^u . D_i) \quad (21)$$

where J^k is the set of jobs that must be processed on machine k.

This lower bound is induced by the fact that all the items of products that have to be processed on a machine k must, sooner or later, be processed on machine k. Splitting jobs into sublots reduces waiting times in front of the machines, but does not prevent jobs from using them. A machine for which LB is attained is called a *critical machine*. This lower bound ignores the sequencing effect. Indeed, one treats the machines "in parallel", *i.e.*, as if they could process two consecutive (in the routing) operations at the same time. Actually, (21) is only an aggregate information about the workload on the machines.

Surprisingly, our experimental study below, shows that this a priori crude lower bound is in fact almost reached in all job-shop cases without set-up time, suggesting that the procedure yields a global optimum.

VI.3   Computational Results

In this section, we present some computational results on two famous examples of job-shop problems in the literature, namely the 10 jobs - 10 machines (10×10) and 6 jobs - 6 machines (6×6) problems, and then on a significant sample of 120 job-shop and flow-shop problems with different parameters and no set-up time. We have also tested the 6×6 and 10×10 problems when set-up times are included. The experiment was conducted on a SUN-4 workstation.

At the scheduling level, the Modified Shifting Bottleneck procedure (MSB) (see Chapter II, and [Dauzere-Peres and Lasserre 93]) is used. This procedure is an improved version of the Shifting Bottleneck procedure proposed by [Adams *et al.* 88]. The iterative procedure is started in Step 3 with given sublot-sizes.

We first consider the example given in [Potts and Baker 89], with 2 jobs and 2 machines in a flow-show (*i.e.*, both jobs are processed first on machine 1, and then on machine 2), and 2 sublots.

Since our modeling is slightly different, data are introduced in a different way, but the example remains the same:

$p_{111} = p_{211} = 1$, $p_{122} = 2$, $p_{222} = 3$.
$D_1 = 7$, $D_2 = 14$.

The initial sublot-sizes are:

$X_{i1} = X_{i2} = D_i/2$, i=1,2

The procedure converges to the optimal value of 57 at iteration 4.

	Initial		Iteration 1		Iteration 2		Iteration 3		Iteration 4	
Sublot-sizes	3.5	7.0	2.333	9.333	2.333	12.444	0.875	12.250	1.0	12.0
	3.5	7.0	4.667	4.667	4.667	1.556	6.125	1.750	6.0	2.0
Makespan	59.50		58.33		58.33		57.75		57.00	

Table VI.1: Potts and Baker example

$X_{11} = 1$, $X_{12} = 6$, $X_{21} = 2$, $X_{22} = 12$.

It is important to note that the optimal sequences on machines 1 and 2 alternate between sublots of product 1 and sublots of product 2.

VI.3.1   The 6×6 and 10×10 Problems

To show the efficiency of the procedure, and more generally of the lot-streaming process, two well-known examples given in [Fisher and Thompson 63] are tested. The first example is a 6 jobs - 6 machines problem with optimal makespan 55. The second example is the famous 10 jobs - 10 machines problem for which the optimal makespan is 930. In both examples $D_i = 1$, $\forall i$. The number of sublots (s) varies from 1 to 6. Initial sublots have equal sizes, i.e., $X_{il} = 1/s$, $\forall i, l$.

We have kept the best makespan after 10 iterations. The results are displayed in Table VI.2 for both problems, and drawn in Figure VI.3.1. On the figure, the straight line represents the lower bound LB given in Section VI.2.6.

Figure VI.3.1 indicates that, in few iterations, the makespan approaches the lower bound as the number of sublots is increased, and therefore the improvement in the makespan tends to 0. Then, it is not necessary to have a very large number of sublots, but rather to make a trade-off between the decrease that one can expect in the makespan and the increase in computing times. Here, 3 or 4 sublots seem sufficient in both cases. That suggests that the procedure is efficient, and seems to provide a (nearly) global rather than a locally optimal solution. This also shows that a very difficult scheduling problem (like the 10×10), may become *easier* if one accepts to eventually split into a (small) number of sublots.

Problem	Lower Bound	Makespan					
	LB	s=1	s=2	s=3	s=4	s=5	s=6
6 jobs, 6 machines	43.00	55.00	46.19	44.31	43.41	43.14	43.03
10 jobs, 10 machines	631.00	950.00	776.64	696.60	672.88	659.93	648.48

Table VI.2: 6×6 and 10×10 problems

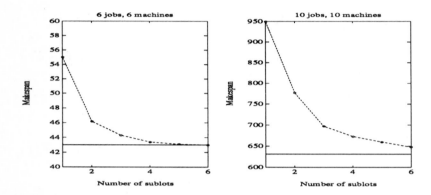

Figure VI-1: Lot streaming for the 6×6 and 10×10 problems

VI.3.2 Test on a Sample

We have also tested our procedure on a sample of 120 problems. For a given number of jobs, 10 problems are randomly generated, *i.e.*,

- the number of machines is randomly generated in a given interval, with a uniform distribution,

- the routing is also randomly generated,

- and the processing times are randomly generated in a given interval using a uniform distribution.

In Tables VI.3-VI.6, we provide the number of jobs, the intervals in which the number of machines and the processing times are randomly generated. For a number of sublots ranging from 1 to 4, we also provide:

- the average (over the 10 problems) relative difference,

- the minimum relative difference,

- and the maximum relative difference

between the makespan and the lower bound.

Number of Jobs	Number of Machines	Processing Times	Number of Sublots	Aver. diff. with LB (%)	Min. diff. with LB (%)	Max. diff. with LB (%)
10	[4,8]	[50,100]	1	18.65	5.22	29.72
			2	2.06	0.00	9.59
			3	0.45	0.00	3.36
			4	0.23	0.00	1.90
		[90,100]	1	16.23	9.78	24.24
			2	1.98	0.00	10.70
			3	0.59	0.00	5.48
			4	0.34	0.00	3.33
		[100,1000]	1	14.70	1.54	22.18
			2	0.97	0.00	5.45
			3	0.15	0.00	1.37
			4	0.05	0.00	0.44
	10	[50,100]	1	32.99	27.87	38.61
			2	11.69	3.55	21.02
			3	5.60	0.00	14.36
			4	3.08	0.00	10.34
		[90,100]	1	38.47	32.87	46.64
			2	17.82	12.11	29.45
			3	11.37	5.43	22.69
			4	8.33	3.29	19.03
		[100,1000]	1	25.71	13.45	32.23
			2	6.56	0.00	13.16
			3	2.25	0.00	6.91
			4	0.97	0.00	5.26
20	[4,8]	[50,100]	1	0.46	0.00	2
			2	0.00	0.00	0.00
			3	0.00	0.00	0.00
			4	0.00	0.00	0.00
		[90,100]	1	2.63	0.00	9.98
			2	0.08	0.00	0.68
			3	0.02	0.00	0.17
			4	0.00	0.00	0.02
		[100,1000]	1	0.52	0.00	1.83
			2	0.00	0.00	0.00
			3	0.00	0.00	0.00
			4	0.00	0.00	0.00

Table VI.3: Job-shop without rounding.

Number of Jobs	Number of Machines	Processing Times	Number of Sublots	Aver. diff. with LB (%)	Min. diff. with LB (%)	Max. diff. with LB (%)
10	[4,8]	[50,100]	1	27.44	19.90	31.76
			2	12.03	8.57	14.60
			3	6.17	3.33	8.27
			4	3.83	1.99	6.38
		[90,100]	1	22.84	16.28	28.78
			2	9.26	4.74	12.98
			3	5.40	1.63	9.05
			4	3.39	0.63	6.39
		[100,1000]	1	25.69	11.38	41.18
			2	8.19	0.79	19.91
			3	3.99	0.11	11.18
			4	2.35	0.02	9.25

Table VI.4: Flow-shop without rounding.

Table VI.3 (resp. Table VI.4) considers job-shop (resp. flow-shop) problems without rounding, whereas Tables VI.5 and VI.6 show the effect of the rounding procedure.

In all the cases, the makespan is very close to the lower bound with only 2, 3, or 4 sublots. $C_{max} \approx LB$ means that the critical machine k (for which the lower bound is obtained) is almost working all the time, *i.e*, there are practically no waiting times between two operations sequenced consecutively on machine k. Thus, the precedence constraints (5') in $LS(S)$ are often (nearly) active, *i.e.*,

$$t_{ijkl} - t_{i'j'kl'} - p^u_{i'j'k}.X_{i'l'} = \epsilon \qquad \forall (o_{i'j'kl'}, o_{ijkl}) \in S \quad (22)$$

where ϵ is a small positive value and is often equal to 0.

Moreover, the first operation in the sequence of k must begin very soon after the beginning of the schedule, and constraint (6) in $LS(S)$ for the last operation o_{ijkl} in the sequence must be nearly active:

$$t_{ijkl} + p^u_{ijk}.X_{il} - C_{max} = \epsilon' \quad (23)$$

where ϵ' is a small positive value.

For job-shop problems (Table VI.3), this result can be explained intuitively by the random choice of the routing of the jobs. Often, some jobs use the critical machine k at the beginning of their routings, and others use it at the end. Thus, there is an operation o_{ijkl} on k with no preceding operation in the routing, and an operation $o_{i'j'kl'}$ with no following operation in the routing. By positioning o_{ijkl} and $o_{i'j'kl'}$ at, respectively, the beginning and the end of the sequence on the critical

Number of Jobs	Number of Machines	Processing Times	Number of Sublots	Average difference with LB (%)				
				No rounding	Rounding			
					10	20	50	100
10	[4,8]	[50,100]	1	18.65	18.65	18.65	18.65	18.65
			2	2.06	3.60	2.75	2.34	2.18
			3	0.45	2.51	1.20	0.74	0.63
			4	0.23	2.93	1.67	0.75	0.44
		[90,100]	1	16.23	16.23	16.23	16.23	16.23
			2	1.98	3.07	2.49	2.17	2.13
			3	0.59	2.81	1.35	0.84	0.84
			4	0.34	2.70	1.52	0.82	0.53
		[100,1000]	1	14.70	14.70	14.70	14.70	14.70
			2	0.97	1.89	1.65	1.23	1.11
			3	0.15	2.33	0.69	0.50	0.27
			4	0.05	2.77	1.06	0.55	0.18
	10	[50,100]	1	32.99	32.99	32.99	32.99	32.99
			2	11.69	13.43	12.44	11.99	11.89
			3	5.60	8.75	7.17	6.09	5.86
			4	3.08	7.78	4.85	3.60	3.37
		[90,100]	1	38.47	38.47	38.47	38.47	38.47
			2	17.82	19.05	18.43	18.06	17.91
			3	11.37	14.54	12.53	11.90	11.61
			4	8.33	11.93	9.85	9.00	8.63
		[100,1000]	1	25.71	25.71	25.71	25.71	25.71
			2	6.56	8.05	7.33	6.79	6.68
			3	2.25	5.81	3.39	2.73	2.52
			4	0.97	4.24	2.72	1.50	1.26
20	[4,8]	[50,100]	1	0.46	0.46	0.46	0.46	0.46
			2	0.00	0.48	0.25	0.08	0.04
			3	0.00	0.36	0.14	0.04	0.04
			4	0.00	0.80	0.39	0.14	0.09
		[90,100]	1	2.63	2.63	2.63	2.63	2.63
			2	0.08	0.72	0.30	0.20	0.11
			3	0.02	0.96	0.50	0.22	0.11
			4	0.00	1.61	0.62	0.24	0.13
		[100,1000]	1	0.52	0.52	0.52	0.52	0.52
			2	0.00	0.62	0.22	0.08	0.05
			3	0.00	0.21	0.27	0.07	0.04
			4	0.00	0.75	0.34	0.12	0.06

Table VI.5: Job-shop with rounding.

Number of Jobs	Number of Machines	Processing Times	Number of Sublots	Average difference with LB (%)				
				No rounding	Rounding			
					10	20	50	100
10	[4,8]	[50,100]	1	27.44	27.44	27.44	27.44	27.44
			2	12.03	13.19	12.58	12.22	12.16
			3	6.17	8.33	7.04	6.50	6.34
			4	3.83	6.69	4.96	4.23	4.04
		[90,100]	1	22.84	22.84	22.84	22.84	22.84
			2	9.26	10.18	9.75	9.48	9.35
			3	5.40	6.88	6.26	5.69	5.59
			4	3.39	5.96	4.48	3.76	3.56
		[100,1000]	1	25.69	25.69	25.69	25.59	25.69
			2	8.19	9.27	8.89	8.39	8.30
			3	3.99	5.98	5.12	4.32	4.15
			4	2.35	4.96	3.74	2.87	2.58

Table VI.6: Flow-shop with rounding.

machine, it is often possible to find sublot-sizes and the remainder of the sequence such that (22) and (23) are satisfied.

For flow-shop problems (Table VI.4), the machines are ordered along the routing of the jobs, *i.e.*, $(o_{ij'k'l}, o_{ijkl}) \in A \Rightarrow k' < k$. In this case, usually, all the operations on the critical machine will have either a preceding operation or a subsequent operation (or both). Therefore, the above comment on job-shop is not valid any more. However, the makespan still approaches the lower bound with very few sublots, although it is never able to reach it. As expected, and in contrast to the job-shop case, a larger number of sublots is needed to improve the makespan.

Tables VI.5 and VI.6 indicate the effect of the (simple) rounding procedure. We consider jobs of 10, 20 50 and 100 items. As expected, the rounding effect is negligible for large jobs, but, surprisingly, it remains small for small jobs.

VI.3.3   With Set-Up Times

Here, we have tested our procedure only on the 6×6 and 10×10 problems already mentionned in Section VI.3.1, and given in [Fisher and Thompson 63]. For each problem, we consider the cases where set-up times are 1%, 10%, 20%, or 50% of the original processing times. Actually, with one lot, the best makespan that can be achieved is the one given by our scheduling procedure on the original problems. We only considered 2 and 3 sublots, since problems with more sublots (*i.e.*, more Boolean variables) cannot be handled by the package we used. In order to compare, we also recall the results without set-up times.

Table VI.7 indicates that, when set-up times are very small (1%), results are

Problem	Lower Bound LB	Percentage of set-up times	Makespan		
			s=1	s=2	s=3
6 jobs, 6 machines	43.00	0%	55.0	46.19	44.31
		1%	55.0	47.19	45.07
		10%	55.0	50.98	51.02
		20%	55.0	53.40	54.40
		50%	55.0	55.0	55.0
10 jobs, 10 machines	631.00	0%	950.0	776.64	696.60
		1%	950.0	781.72	710.08
		10%	950.0	848.01	841.63
		20%	950.0	926.28	922.34
		50%	950.0	951.0	982.0

Table VI.7: 6 × 6 and 10 × 10 with set-up time

close to the no set-up case for 2 and 3 sublots per job. Nevertheless, in nearly all the other cases, the best result is found with $s = 2$. When $s = 2$, with 1% and 10% in the first problem, and with 1%, 10% and 20% in the second problem, almost every sublot is non-empty. Hence, Boolean variables in $LS_{set}(S)$ can be set to 1 to simplify the resolution.

VI.3.4   CPU Time and Number of Iterations

In all the examples we have recorded the best solution obtained after 10 iterations. However, a very good solution is always obtained after very few iterations whereas the improvement in the last iterations is marginal. In Tables VI.8-VI.10, one finds

- the average number of iterations to reach the best solution for the job-shop and flow-shop cases.

- the average relative difference between the best solution and the solutions obtained at the first and second iterations

The conclusion is that 2 iterations are well enough to obtain a solution close to the best one and this is even more true when the number of jobs increases.

Concerning the CPU time, most of the computational effort is spent in the scheduling algorithm. Table VI.11 shows the mean CPU time in seconds per iteration on a SUN-4 workstation. Actually, based on the previous remark about the sufficient number of iterations, the computing time can be greatly reduced by stopping the procedure at the end of the second iteration.

Number of Jobs	Number of Machines	Processing Times	Number of Sublots	Aver. nb. of iter.	Min. nb. of iter.	Max. nb. of iter.
10	[4,8]	[50,100]	2	2.8	1	10
			3	3.3	1	8
			4	3.5	1	10
		[90,100]	2	3.6	1	7
			3	2.8	1	9
			4	2.6	1	9
		[100,1000]	2	2.9	1	10
			3	3.3	1	10
			4	2.4	1	7
	10	[50,100]	2	5.4	1	10
			3	5.2	1	10
			4	3.7	1	9
		[90,100]	2	6.0	3	10
			3	6.2	1	10
			4	4.3	1	10
		[100,1000]	2	4.3	1	9
			3	5.6	1	10
			4	6.3	1	10
20	[4,8]	[50,100]	2	1.0	1	1
			3	1.0	1	1
			4	1.0	1	1
		[90,100]	2	2.5	1	10
			3	1.8	1	5
			4	1.9	1	7
		[100,1000]	2	1.9	1	10
			3	1.3	1	4
			4	1.1	1	2

Table VI.8: Job-shop, number of iterations.

Number of Jobs	Number of Machines	Processing Times	Number of Sublots	Aver. nb. of iter.	Min. nb. of iter.	Max. nb. of iter.
10	[4,8]	[50,100]	2	6.4	2	10
			3	6.3	4	8
			4	6.8	4	10
		[90,100]	2	6.6	3	9
			3	5.9	2	10
			4	5.7	2	10
		[100,1000]	2	7.1	1	10
			3	5.9	2	10
			4	5.6	2	10

Table VI.9: Flow-shop, number of iterations.

Number of Jobs	Number of Machines	Processing Times	Number of Sublots	Aver. diff. with iteration 1 (%)		Aver. diff. with iteration 1 or 2 (%)	
				Job-shop	Flow-shop	Job-shop	Flow-shop
10	[4,8]	[50,100]	2	0.82	2.14	0.25	1.15
			3	0.34	2.55	0.16	1.30
			4	0.37	2.34	0.14	1.54
		[90,100]	2	0.72	2.35	0.44	1.31
			3	0.50	2.42	0.10	0.91
			4	0.42	2.15	0.10	0.96
		[100,1000]	2	1.12	2.92	0.42	1.56
			3	0.54	3.56	0.26	1.05
			4	0.34	3.48	0.01	0.76
	10	[50,100]	2	1.09	-	0.83	-
			3	0.83	-	0.68	-
			4	0.84	-	0.43	-
		[90,100]	2	2.51	-	1.83	-
			3	1.59	-	1.26	-
			4	1.08	-	0.52	-
		[100,1000]	2	2.28	-	0.94	-
			3	1.05	-	0.57	-
			4	1.03	-	0.81	-
20	[4,8]	[50,100]	2	0.00	-	0.00	-
			3	0.00	-	0.00	-
			4	0.00	-	0.00	-
		[90,100]	2	0.37	-	0.11	-
			3	0.14	-	0.01	-
			4	0.05	-	0.00	-
		[100,1000]	2	0.04	-	0.01	-
			3	0.02	-	0.00	-
			4	0.01	-	0.00	-

Table VI.10: Average difference with first iterations.

Number of Jobs	Number of Machines	Processing Times	Number of Sublots	Mean Time per Iteration (Sec.)	
				Job-shop	Flow-shop
10	[4,8]	[50,100]	1	18	16
			2	59	42
			3	142	85
			4	300	148
		[90,100]	1	19	14
			2	66	33
			3	145	72
			4	252	126
		[100,1000]	1	13	14
			2	31	34
			3	62	65
			4	117	116
	10	[50,100]	1	33	-
			2	163	-
			3	656	-
			4	1628	-
		[90,100]	1	32	-
			2	176	-
			3	702	-
			4	1827	-
		[100,1000]	1	32	-
			2	146	-
			3	425	-
			4	863	-
20	[4,8]	[50,100]	1	56	-
			2	173	-
			3	455	-
			4	1137	-
		[90,100]	1	61	-
			2	245	-
			3	773	-
			4	1720	-
		[100,1000]	1	42	-
			2	128	-
			3	318	-
			4	654	-

Table VI.11: Mean time per iteration.

VI.4   Impact on Lotsizing Models

As discussed in Chapters I and III, a traditional hierarchical approach in Production Planning consists of first computing a production plan before sending this production plan as input data to a scheduling level. With such an approach nothing guarantees that the plan actually computed is feasible, *i.e.*, that there exists a schedule to achieve that plan. By this, we mean that the products that must be finished in a certain quantity at the end of some period in the discretized lotsizing model, are actually finished by this due date with this schedule.

In most discrete-time capacitated lotsizing models (*Master Production Schedule* for example), the capacity constraints are aggregate (see [Salomon 91]). They just state that a machine cannot work more than the time available in each period. It is an aggregate information on the workload of the machines and the sequencing of lots on the machines is totally ignored. For a given period in the discretized horizon, this capacity constraint, when evaluated for some values $\{D_i\}$ of the lots, is precisely the lower bound (21).

Therefore, suppose that a Master Production Schedule is solved. The output consists of lot-sizes $\{D_{it}\}$ for each product $i = 1,..,n$ and each time period $t = 1,..,T$. The capacity constraint just states that the time spent on each machine at each period does not exceed the amount of time each machine is available in the period, *i.e.*, for each period, the lower bound (21) is less than or equal to, for example, the number of hours in the period.

What our experimental results suggest is that the production plan is actually *nearly* achievable **provided** a good **lot-streaming** procedure is available at the scheduling level.

In other words, those results somehow validate the hierarchical approach where the lotsizing models **ignore** the **detailed** capacity constraints induced by the sequencing of operations on the machines. However, it should be noted that our lot-streaming procedure uses a sophisticated scheduling algorithm. It is not obvious at all that a more naive scheduling procedure would yield the same conclusions.

VI.5   Conclusion

We have proposed an integrated lot-streaming model for the general job-shop case, and an iterative procedure to solve the problem. It is worth noting that, even if we have considered the makespan criterion, the methodology can be easily generalized to many other types of criteria, and extended to include other constraints.

Numerical experiments on a significant sample show the great improvements that can be achieved with a lot-streaming procedure, especially in the no set-up case. In this case, in few iterations, the makespan comes close to a lower bound with few sublots, suggesting that the procedure yields a nearly global optimum. Moreover, the procedure is not very sensitive to the size of the jobs, and to the rounding procedure which derives integer-valued sublot sizes. When set-up times are considered and after few sublots, the makespan is no longer decreasing, indicating that a small number of sublots is also sufficient.

Last but not least, the impact of this experiment on capacitated lotsizing models has been discussed. In these models, the aggregate capacity constraint takes the workload on the machines into account and ignore the sequencing of operations. Our experimental results indicate that this aggregate modeling might be relevant **provided** one can split the computed lots into enough sublots (actually very few) and a good lot-streaming procedure is available.

*

*   *

Conclusion

As already noted in the Introduction, the consistency issue between the planning and scheduling decisions is mentioned as a crucial issue in Production Management. Despite its importance, few works have addressed this issue and to our knowledge, so far, no planning model really ensures the existence of a schedule compatible with the production plan, *i.e.,* such that the plan is achievable. The integrated model for planning and scheduling presented in this book, as well as the solving procedure, are new, and are one of the first steps in this direction.

Our hope is that this work will motivate extensions of the model, or other approaches to address this crucial consistency issue.

At the scheduling level, an improved version of the shifting bottleneck procedure has been presented and tested. Actually, an algorithm for the general one-machine problem with dependent jobs has been proposed. Finally, we have also presented an integrated model, and a solving procedure, for the job-shop scheduling problem with lot streaming, *i.e.,* when lots can be splitted in to sublots. Again, very few results are available in the literature for this difficult problem. To our knowledge, this procedure is the first to handle the general job-shop case. Despite its simplicity, it demonstrates that significant improvements in scheduling can be expected when lot streaming is possible. The potential impact of these results on capacitated lotsizing models has also been discussed.

Bibliography

[Adams *et al.* 88] J. ADAMS, E. BALAS, D. ZAWACK (1988). The Shifting Bottleneck Procedure for Job Shop Scheduling. *Management Sci. 34*, 391-401.

[Afentakis 85] P. AFENTAKIS (1985). Simultaneous Lot Sizing and Sequencing for Multistage Production Systems. *IIE Transactions 17*, 327-331.

[Aggarwal 91] S. AGGARWAL (1991). Evolution or Revolution in Materials Managament. *Joint ORSA/TIMS national meeting*, may 12-15, 1991, Nashville, Tennessee.

[Anthony 65] R.N. ANTHONY (1965). *Planning and Control Systems : A Framework for Analysis.* Harvard University, Graduate Schoole of Business Administration, Cambridge, Massachusetts.

[Balas 69] E. BALAS (1969). Machine Sequencing via Disjunctive Graphs. *Oper. Res. 17*, 941-957.

[Baker 74] K.R. BAKER (1974). *Introduction to Sequencing and Scheduling*, Wiley, New-York.

[Baker 87] K.R. BAKER (1987). Lot streaming to Reduce Cycle Time in a Flow Shop, *Working Paper n⁰ 203*, Amos Tuck School, Dartmouth College.

[Baker and Pyke 90] K.R. BAKER, D.F. PYKE (1990). Solution Procedures for the Lot-Streaming Problem. *Decision Sciences 21*, 475-491.

[Barker and Mc Mahon 85] J.R. BARKER, G.B. Mc MAHON (1985). Scheduling the General Job-Shop. *Management Sci. 31*, 594-598.

[Bénassy 87] J. BENASSY (1987). *La gestion de production*, Hermès.

[Bitran and Tirupati 93] G.R. BITRAN, and D. TIRUPATI (1993). Hierarchical Production Planning. S.C. GRAVES, A.H.G. RINNOOY KAN, P.H. ZIPKIN (eds.) (1993). *Logistics of Production and Inventory*, Handbooks in Op. Res. and Man. Sci., Vol. 4, North-Holland.

[Bratley et al. 73] P. BRATLEY, M. FLORIAN et P. ROBILLARD (1973). On Sequencing With Earliest Starts and Due Dates with Application to Computing Bounds for the $(n/m/G/F_{max})$ Problem. *Naval Res. Logist. Quart.* *20*, 57-67.

[Brucker 91] G. BRUCKER (1991). New Job-Shop Scheduling Algorithms. *EURO XI Conference*, Aachen 1991.

[Buxey 89] G. BUXEY (1989). Production Scheduling : Practice and Theory. *European J. of Op. Res.* *39*, 17-31.

[Carlier 78] J. CARLIER (1978). Ordonnancements à Contraintes Disjonctives. *RAIRO 12*, 333-351.

[Carlier 82] J. CARLIER (1982). The One-Machine Sequencing Problem. *European J. of Oper. Res. 11*, 42-47.

[Carlier and Chrétienne 88] J. CARLIER, P. CHRETIENNE (1988). *Problèmes d'Ordonnancement - Modélisation / Complexité / Algorithmes*, ERI, Masson.

[Carlier and Pinson 89] J. CARLIER, E. PINSON (1989). An Algorithm for Solving the Job-shop Problem. *Management Sci. 35*, 164-176.

[Conway *et al.* 67] R.W. CONWAY, W.L. MAXWELL, L.W. MILLER (1967). *Theory of Scheduling*, Addison-Wesley, Reading.

[Dauzere-Peres 90] S. DAUZERE-PERES (1990). A procedure for the one-machine sequencing problem with dependent jobs. LAAS Report n° 90382 (November 1990), accepted in *Eur. J. Oper. Res.*.

[Dauzere-Peres 92] S. DAUZERE-PERES (1992). *Planification et Ordonnancement de la Production: Une Approche Intégrée Cohérente*, Thèse de Doctorat de l'Université Paul Sabatier. Toulouse. LAAS Report n° 92129 (March 1992).

[Dauzere-Peres and Lasserre 93] S. DAUZERE-PERES, J.B. LASSERRE (1993). A Modified Shifting Bottleneck Procedure for Job Shop Scheduling. *Int. J. of Prod. Res. 31*, 923-932

[Dauzere-Peres and Lasserre 94] S. DAUZERE-PERES, J.B. LASSERRE (1994). Integration of Lotsizing and Scheduling Decisions in a Job-Shop, *Eur. J. Oper. Res.* To appear.

[Elmaghraby 78] S.E. ELMAGHRABY (1978). The Economic Lot Scheduling Problem (ELSP) : Review and Extensions. *Management Sci. 24*, 587-598.

[Fisher and Thompson 63] H. FISHER, G.L. THOMPSON (1963). Probabilistic Learning Combinations of Local Job-Shop Scheduling Rules. J.F. MUTH, G.L. THOMPSON (eds.) (1963). *Industrial Scheduling*, Prentice-Hall, Englewood Cliffs, NJ, 225-251.

[Fontan and Imbert 85] G. FONTAN, S. IMBERT (1985). Interaction between the Two Levels of Decision Making in a Job Shop. *EURO VI Conference*, Bologne 1985.

[Garey *et al.* 81] M.R. GAREY, D.S. JOHNSON, B.B. SIMONS, R.E. TARJAN (1981). Scheduling Unit-Time Tasks with Arbitrary Release Times and Deadlines. *SIAM J. Comput. 10*, 256-269.

[Gershwin 89] S.B. GERSHWIN (1989). Hierarchical Flow Control : A Framework for Scheduling and Planning Discrete Events in Manufacturing Systems. *Proceedings of the IEEE 77*, 195-209.

[Giard 88] V. GIARD (1988). *Gestion de la Production - 2^{ieme} édition*, Gestion, Economica.

[Giffler and Thompson 60] B. GIFFLER, G.L. THOMPSON (1960). Algorithms for Solving Production-Scheduling Problems. *Oper. Res. 8*, 487-503.

[Golhar and Stamm 91] D.Y. GOLHAR, C.L. STAMM (1991). The Just-In-Time Philosophy : A Literature Review. *Int. J. Prod. Res. 29*, 657-676.

[Goyal 76] S.K. GOYAL (1976). Note on "Manufacturing Cycle Time Determination for a Multi-Stage Economic Production Quantity Model". *Management Sci. 23*, 332-333.

[Hax and Candea 84] A.C. HAX, D. CANDEA (1984). *Production and Inventory Management*, Prentice Hall, Englewoods Cliffs, New Jersey.

[Horn 74] W.A. HORN (1974). Some Simple Scheduling Algorithms. *Naval Res. Logist. Quart. 21*, 177-185.

[Karmarkar 87] U.S. KARMARKAR (1987). Lot-Sizing and Sequencing Delays. *Management Sci. 33*, 419-423.

[Kropp and Smunt 90] D.H. KROPP, T.L. SMUNT (1990). Optimal and Heuristic Models for Lot Splitting in a Flow Shop. *Decision Sciences 21*, 691-709.

[Lageweg *et al.* 76] B.J. LAGEWEG, J.K. LENSTRA, A.H.G. RINNOOY KAN (1976). Minimizing Maximum Lateness on One Machine : Computational Experience and Some Applications. *Statis. Neerlandica 30*, 25-41.

[Lageweg *et al.* 77] B.J. LAGEWEG, J.K. LENSTRA, A.H.G. RINNOOY KAN (1977). Job-Shop Scheduling by Implicit Enumeration. *Management Sci.* *24*, 441-450.

[Lasserre 92] J.B. LASSERRE (1992). An Integrated Model for Job-Shop Planning and Scheduling. *Management Sci. 38*, 1201-1211.

[Lawler *et al.* 93] E.L. LAWLER, J.K. LENSTRA, A.H.G. RINNOOY KAN, D.B. SHMOYS (1993). Sequencing and Scheduling: Algorithms and Complexity. S.C. GRAVES, A.H.G. RINNOOY KAN, P.H. ZIPKIN (eds.) (1993). *Logistics of Production and Inventory*, Handbooks in Op. Res. and Man. Sci., Vol. 4, North-Holland.

[Lenstra *et al.* 77] J.K. LENSTRA, A.H.G. RINNOOY KAN, P. BRUCKER (1977). Complexity of Machine Scheduling Problems. *Ann. Discrete Math. I*, 343-362.

[Lenstra and Rinnooy Kan 84] J.K. LENSTRA, A.H.G. RINNOOY KAN (1984). New Directions in Scheduling Theory. *Oper. Res. Letters 6*, 255-259.

[Mc Mahon and Florian 75] G. MC MAHON, M. FLORIAN (1975). On Scheduling with Ready Times and Due Dates to Minimize Maximum Lateness. *Oper. Res. 23*, 475-482.

[Merce 87] C. MERCE (1987). *Cohérence des décisions en planification hiérarchisée.* Thèse de docteur d'état, Université Paul Sabatier, Toulouse.

[Montazeri and Van Wassenhove 90] M. MONTAZERI, L.N. VAN WASSENHOVE (1990). Analysis of Scheduling Rules for an FMS. *Int. J. of Prod. Res. 28*, 785-802.

[Orlicky 75] J.A. ORLICKY (1975). *Material Requirement Planning: The New Way of Life in Production and Inventory Management.* McGraw Hill, New-York.

[Potts and Baker 89] C.N. POTTS, K.R. BAKER (1989). Flow Shop Scheduling with Lot Streaming. *Oper. Res. Letters 8*, 297-303.

[Potts and Van Wassenhove 92] C.N. POTTS, L.N. VAN WASSENHOVE (1992). Integrating Scheduling with Batching and Lot-Sizing : a Review of Algorithms and Complexity. *J. of the Oper. Res. Soc. 43*, 395-406.

[Rinnooy Kan 76] A.H.G. RINNOOY KAN (1976). *Machine Scheduling Problems : Classification, Complexity and Computations*, Nijhoff, The Hague.

[Roy and Sussman 64] B. ROY, B. SUSSMAN (1964). *Les Problèmes d'Ordonnancement avec Contraintes Disjonctives*, Note DS n° 9 bis, SEMA, Montrouge.

[Salomon 91] M. SALOMON (1991). *Deterministic Lotsizing Models for Production Planning*, Lecture Notes in Economics and Mathematical Systems, Springer-Verlag, Heidelberg.

[Smith 78] D.J. SMITH (1978). Material Requirement Planning, in A.C Hax (editor), *Studies in Operations Management*, North Holland, Amsterdam.

[Szendrovits 75] A.Z. SZENDROVITS (1975). Manufacturing Cycle Time Determination for a Multi-Stage Economic Production Quantity Model. *Management Sci. 22*, 298-308.

[Szendrovits 76] A.Z. SZENDROVITS (1976). On the Optimality of Sub-Batch Sizes for a Multi-Stage EPQ Model - A Rejoinder. *Management Sci. 23*, 334-338

[Taillard 89] E. TAILLARD (1989). *Parallel Taboo Search Technique for the Jobshop Scheduling Problem*, ORWP 89/11, DMA, Ecole Polytechnique Fédérale de Lausanne, Lausanne.

[Triesch 87] D. TRIETSCH (1987). Optimal Transfer Lots for Batch Manufacturing, manuscript presented at the *ORSA/TIMS Conference*, St. Louis.

[Van Laarhoven et al. 92] P.J.M. VAN LAARHOVEN, E.H.L. AARTS, J.K. LENSTRA (1992). Job Shop Scheduling by Simulated Annealing, *Oper. Res. 40*, 113-125.

[Vollmann et al. 84] T.E. VOLLMANN, W.L. BERRY, D. C. WHYBARK (1984). *Manufacturing Planning and Control Systems*, Dow Jones-Irving, Homewood, Illinois.

[Zdrzalka and Grabowski 89] S. ZDRZALKA, J. GRABOWSKI (1989). An Algorithm for Single Machine Sequencing with Release Dates to Minimize Maximum Cost. *Discrete Applied Math. 23*, 73-89.

[Zipkin 91] P.H. ZIPKIN (1991). Computing Optimal Lot Sizes in the Economic Lot Scheduling Problem. *Oper. Res. 39*, 56-63.

List of Figures

I-1   Interactions between management system, production system and environment.   3
I-2   Three-level decision structure.   4
I-3   Typical production planning approach.   7
I-4   Iterative procedure.   14
I-5   A simple kanban system   16

II-1   Disjunctive graph.   19
II-2   Graph with choice of a complete selection.   20
II-3   Gantt charts.   21
II-4   Disjunctive graph.   30
II-5   Disjunctive graph with selections S_2 and S_4.   31

III-1   Disjunctive graph.   49
III-2   Planning problem.   50
III-3   Multi-period scheduling.   53
III-4   Representation of due dates.   54

IV-1   Global scheduling policy.   73
IV-2   Gantt chart in the global scheduling policy.   74
IV-3   Introduction of fictitious arcs.   75
IV-4   Introduction of fictitious nodes.   75
IV-5   Global scheduling policy; MSB procedure.   77
IV-6   Global scheduling policy; MSB procedure with modification.   78
IV-7   Global scheduling policy; MSB procedure. Final costs with and without the modification.   79
IV-8   Global scheduling policy; MSB procedure and PRD heuristic.   81
IV-9   Global scheduling policy. Final costs with the two scheduling methods.   82
IV-10   Period by period scheduling policy.   83
IV-11   Gantt chart in the period by period scheduling policy.   84
IV-12   Period by period scheduling policy; MSB procedure.   85
IV-13   Period by period scheduling policy; MSB procedure with modification.   86
IV-14   Period by period scheduling policy; MSB procedure. Final costs with and without modification.   87

IV-15 Period by period scheduling policy; MSB procedure and PRD heuristic. 89

IV-16 Period by period scheduling policy. Final costs with the two scheduling methods. 90

IV-17 Final costs with the two scheduling methods, and in the two policies. 91

IV-18 Planning on a rolling horizon. 94

V-1   WIP inventories. 101

VI-1   Lot streaming for the 6×6 and 10×10 problems 116

List of Tables

II.1   Comparison between CAR and DEP. 38
II.2   Comparison between SB1, SB2, and MSB. 41

III.1 6-6 job-shop scheduling problem 66
III.2 Fixed routing and processing times; no set-up time; different initial plans 67
III.3 Fixed routing and processing times; set-up times; different initial plans. 68
III.4 Fixed routing and initial plan; no set-up time; random processing times. 69
III.5 Fixed initial plan; no set-up time; random routing and processing times. 69

IV.1   Global scheduling policy; MSB procedure. 76
IV.2   Global scheduling policy; MSB procedure with modification. . . . 78
IV.3   Global scheduling policy; PRD heuristic. 80
IV.4   Period by period scheduling policy; MSB procedure. 85
IV.5   Period by period scheduling policy; PRD heuristic. 88
IV.6   Global scheduling policy; MSB procedure. 93

V.1   Subcontracting option. $c_{it}^{st} = 10, \quad \forall i,t.$ 100
V.2   Subcontracting option. $c_{it}^{st} = 10 \quad \forall i,t.$ 101
V.3   WIP inventories. $c_{it}^{int} = 0.01 \quad \forall i,t.$ 104
V.4   WIP Inventories. $c_{it}^{int} = 1.0 \quad \forall i,t.$ 105

VI.1   Potts and Baker example 115
VI.2 6×6 and 10×10 problems 116
VI.3   Job-shop without rounding. 117
VI.4   Flow-shop without rounding. 118
VI.5   Job-shop with rounding. 119
VI.6   Flow-shop with rounding. 120
VI.7 6×6 and 10×10 with set-up time 121
VI.8   Job-shop, number of iterations. 122
VI.9   Flow-shop, number of iterations. 122
VI.10 Average difference with first iterations. 123
VI.11 Mean time per iteration. 124

Springer-Verlag
and the Environment

We at Springer-Verlag firmly believe that an international science publisher has a special obligation to the environment, and our corporate policies consistently reflect this conviction.

We also expect our business partners – paper mills, printers, packaging manufacturers, etc. – to commit themselves to using environmentally friendly materials and production processes.

The paper in this book is made from low- or no-chlorine pulp and is acid free, in conformance with international standards for paper permanency.

Lecture Notes in Economics and Mathematical Systems

For information about Vols. 1–234
please contact your bookseller or Springer-Verlag

Vol. 235: Stochastic Models in Reliability Theory Proceedings, 1984. Edited by S. Osaki and Y. Hatoyama. VII, 212 pages. 1984.

Vol. 236: G. Gandolfo, P.C. Padoan, A Disequilibrium Model of Real and Financial Accumulation in an Open Economy. VI, 172 pages. 1984.

Vol. 237: Misspecification Analysis. Proceedings, 1983. Edited by T.K. Dijkstra. V, 129 pages. 1984.

Vol. 238: W. Domschke, A. Drexl, Location and Layout Planning. IV, 134 pages. 1985.

Vol. 239: Microeconomic Models of Housing Markets. Edited by K. Stahl. VII, 197 pages. 1985.

Vol. 240: Contributions to Operations Research. Proceedings, 1984. Edited by K. Neumann and D. Pallaschke. V, 190 pages. 1985.

Vol. 241: U. Wittmann, Das Konzept rationaler Preiserwartungen. XI, 310 Seiten. 1985.

Vol. 242: Decision Making with Multiple Objectives. Proceedings, 1984. Edited by Y.Y. Haimes and V. Chankong. XI, 571 pages. 1985.

Vol. 243: Integer Programming and Related Areas. A Classified Bibliography 1981–1984. Edited by R. von Randow. XX, 386 pages. 1985.

Vol. 244: Advances in Equilibrium Theory. Proceedings, 1984. Edited by C.D. Aliprantis, O. Burkinshaw and N.J. Rothman. II, 235 pages. 1985.

Vol. 245: J.E.M. Wilhelm, Arbitrage Theory. VII, 114 pages. 1985.

Vol. 246: P.W. Otter, Dynamic Feature Space Modelling, Filtering and Self-Tuning Control of Stochastic·Systems. XIV, 177 pages.1985.

Vol. 247: Optimization and Discrete Choice in Urban Systems. Proceedings, 1983. Edited by B.G. Hutchinson, P. Nijkamp and M. Batty Vl, 371 pages. 1985.

Vol. 248: Pural Rationality and Interactive Decision Processes. Proceedings, 1984. Edited by M. Grauer, M. Thompson and A.P. Wierzbicki. VI, 354 pages. 1985.

Vol. 249: Spatial Price Equilibrium: Advances in Theory, Computation and Application. Proceedings, 1984. Edited by P.T. Harker. VII, 277 pages. 1985.

Vol. 250: M. Roubens, Ph. Vincke, Preference Modelling. VIII, 94 pages. 1985.

Vol. 251: Input-Output Modeling. Proceedings, 1984. Edited by A. Smyshlyaev. VI, 261 pages. 1985.

Vol. 252: A. Birolini, On the Use of Stochastic Processes in Modeling Reliability Problems. VI, 105 pages. 1985.

Vol. 253: C. Withagen, Economic Theory and International Trade in Natural Exhaustible Resources. VI, 172 pages. 1985.

Vol. 254: S. Müller, Arbitrage Pricing of Contingent Claims. VIII, 151 pages. 1985.

Vol. 255: Nondifferentiable Optimization: Motivations and Applications. Proceedings, 1984. Edited by V.F. Demyanov and D. Pallaschke. VI, 350 pages. 1985.

Vol. 256: Convexity and Duality in Optimization. Proceedings, 1984. Edited by J. Ponstein. V, 142 pages. 1985.

Vol. 257: Dynamics of Macrosystems. Proceedings, 1984. Edited by J.-P. Aubin, D. Saari and K. Sigmund. VI, 280 pages. 1985.

Vol. 258: H. Funke, Eine allgemeine Theorie der Polypol- und Oligopolpreisbildung. III, 237 pages. 1985.

Vol. 259: Infinite Programming. Proceedings, 1984. Edited by E.J. Anderson and A.B. Philpott. XIV, 244 pages. 1985.

Vol. 260: H.-J. Kruse, Degeneracy Graphs and the Neighbourhood Problem. VIII, 128 pages. 1986.

Vol. 261: Th.R. Gulledge, Jr., N.K. Womer, The Economics of Made-to-Order Production. VI, 134 pages. 1986.

Vol. 262: H.U. Buhl, A Neo-Classical Theory of Distribution and Wealth. V, 146 pages. 1986.

Vol. 263: M. Schäfer, Resource Extraction and Market Struucture. XI, 154 pages. 1986.

Vol. 264: Models of Economic Dynamics. Proceedings, 1983. Edited by H.F. Sonnenschein. VII, 212 pages. 1986.

Vol. 265: Dynamic Games and Applications in Economics. Edited by T. Basar. IX, 288 pages. 1986.

Vol. 266: Multi-Stage Production Planning and Inventory Control. Edited by S. Axsäter, Ch. Schneeweiss and E. Silver. V, 264 pages.1986.

Vol. 267: R. Bemelmans, The Capacity Aspect of Inventories. IX, 165 pages. 1986.

Vol. 268: V. Firchau, Information Evaluation in Capital Markets. VII, 103 pages. 1986.

Vol. 269: A. Borglin, H. Keiding, Optimality in Infinite Horizon Economies. VI, 180 pages. 1986.

Vol. 270: Technological Change, Employment and Spatial Dynamics. Proceedings, 1985. Edited by P. Nijkamp. VII, 466 pages. 1986.

Vol. 271: C. Hildreth, The Cowles Commission in Chicago, 1939–1955. V, 176 pages. 1986.

Vol. 272: G. Clemenz, Credit Markets with Asymmetric Information. VIII,212 pages. 1986.

Vol. 273: Large-Scale Modelling and Interactive Decision Analysis. Proceedings, 1985. Edited by G. Fandel, M. Grauer, A. Kurzhanski and A.P. Wierzbicki. VII, 363 pages. 1986.

Vol. 274: W.K. Klein Haneveld, Duality in Stochastic Linear and Dynamic Programming. VII, 295 pages. 1986.

Vol. 275: Competition, Instability, and Nonlinear Cycles. Proceedings, 1985. Edited by W. Semmler. XII, 340 pages. 1986.

Vol. 276: M.R. Baye, D.A. Black, Consumer Behavior, Cost of Living Measures, and the Income Tax. VII, 119 pages. 1986.

Vol. 277: Studies in Austrian Capital Theory, Investment and Time. Edited by M. Faber. VI, 317 pages. 1986.

Vol. 278: W.E. Diewert, The Measurement of the Economic Benefits of Infrastructure Services. V, 202 pages. 1986.

Vol. 279: H.-J. Büttler, G. Frei and B. Schips, Estimation of Disequilibrium Modes. VI, 114 pages. 1986.

Vol. 280: H.T. Lau, Combinatorial Heuristic Algorithms with FORTRAN. VII, 126 pages. 1986.

Vol. 281: Ch.-L. Hwang, M.-J. Lin, Group Decision Making under Multiple Criteria. XI, 400 pages. 1987.

Vol. 282: K. Schittkowski, More Test Examples for Nonlinear Programming Codes. V, 261 pages. 1987.

Vol. 283: G. Gabisch, H.-W. Lorenz, Business Cycle Theory. VII, 229 pages. 1987.

Vol. 284: H. Lütkepohl, Forecasting Aggregated Vector ARMA Processes. X, 323 pages. 1987.

Vol. 285: Toward Interactive and Intelligent Decision Support Systems. Volume 1. Proceedings, 1986. Edited by Y. Sawaragi, K. Inoue and H. Nakayama. XII, 445 pages. 1987.

Vol. 286: Toward Interactive and Intelligent Decision Support Systems. Volume 2. Proceedings, 1986. Edited by Y. Sawaragi, K. Inoue and H. Nakayama. XII, 450 pages. 1987.

Vol. 287: Dynamical Systems. Proceedings, 1985. Edited by A.B. Kurzhanski and K. Sigmund. VI, 215 pages. 1987.

Vol. 288: G.D. Rudebusch, The Estimation of Macroeconomic Disequilibrium Models with Regime Classification Information. VII,128 pages. 1987.

Vol. 289: B.R. Meijboom, Planning in Decentralized Firms. X, 168 pages. 1987.

Vol. 290: D.A. Carlson, A. Haurie, Infinite Horizon Optimal Control. XI, 254 pages. 1987.

Vol. 291: N. Takahashi, Design of Adaptive Organizations. VI, 140 pages. 1987.

Vol. 292: I. Tchijov, L. Tomaszewicz (Eds.), Input-Output Modeling. Proceedings, 1985. VI, 195 pages. 1987.

Vol. 293: D. Batten, J. Casti, B. Johansson (Eds.), Economic Evolution and Structural Adjustment. Proceedings, 1985. VI, 382 pages.

Vol. 294: J. Jahn, W. Knabs (Eds.), Recent Advances and Historical Development of Vector Optimization. VII, 405 pages. 1987.

Vol. 295. H. Meister, The Purification Problem for Constrained Games with Incomplete Information. X, 127 pages. 1987.

Vol. 296: A. Börsch-Supan, Econometric Analysis of Discrete Choice. VIII, 211 pages. 1987.

Vol. 297: V. Fedorov, H. Läuter (Eds.), Model-Oriented Data Analysis. Proceedings, 1987. VI, 239 pages. 1988.

Vol. 298: S.H. Chew, Q. Zheng, Integral Global Optimization. VII, 179 pages. 1988.

Vol. 299: K. Marti, Descent Directions and Efficient Solutions in Discretely Distributed Stochastic Programs. XIV, 178 pages. 1988.

Vol. 300: U. Derigs, Programming in Networks and Graphs. XI, 315 pages. 1988.

Vol. 301: J. Kacprzyk, M. Roubens (Eds.), Non-Conventional Preference Relations in Decision Making. VII, 155 pages. 1988.

Vol. 302: H.A. Eiselt, G. Pederzoli (Eds.), Advances in Optimization and Control. Proceedings, 1986. VIII, 372 pages. 1988.

Vol. 303: F.X. Diebold, Empirical Modeling of Exchange Rate Dynamics. VII, 143 pages. 1988.

Vol. 304: A. Kurzhanski, K. Neumann, D. Pallaschke (Eds.), Optimization, Parallel Processing and Applications. Proceedings, 1987. VI, 292 pages. 1988.

Vol. 305: G.-J.C.Th. van Schijndel, Dynamic Firm and Investor Behaviour under Progressive Personal Taxation. X, 215 pages.1988.

Vol. 306: Ch. Klein, A Static Microeconomic Model of Pure Competition. VIII, 139 pages. 1988.

Vol. 307: T.K. Dijkstra (Ed.), On Model Uncertainty and its Statistical Implications. VII, 138 pages. 1988.

Vol. 308: J.R. Daduna, A. Wren (Eds.), Computer-Aided Transit Scheduling. VIII, 339 pages. 1988.

Vol. 309: G. Ricci, K. Velupillai (Eds.), Growth Cycles and Multisectoral Economics: the Goodwin Tradition. III, 126 pages. 1988.

Vol. 310: J. Kacprzyk, M. Fedrizzi (Eds.), Combining Fuzzy Imprecision with Probabilistic Uncertainty in Decision Making. IX, 399 pages. 1988.

Vol. 311: R. Färe, Fundamentals of Production Theory. IX, 163 pages. 1988.

Vol. 312: J. Krishnakumar, Estimation of Simultaneous Equation Models with Error Components Structure. X, 357 pages. 1988.

Vol. 313: W. Jammernegg, Sequential Binary Investment Decisions. VI, 156 pages. 1988.

Vol. 314: R. Tietz, W. Albers, R. Selten (Eds.), Bounded Rational Behavior in Experimental Games and Markets. VI, 368 pages. 1988.

Vol. 315: I. Orishimo, G.J.D. Hewings, P. Nijkamp (Eds), Information Technology: Social and Spatial Perspectives. Proceedings 1986. VI, 268 pages. 1988.

Vol. 316: R.L. Basmann, D.J. Slottje, K. Hayes, J.D. Johnson, D.J. Molina, The Generalized Fechner-Thurstone Direct Utility Function and Some of its Uses. VIII, 159 pages. 1988.

Vol. 317: L. Bianco, A. La Bella (Eds.), Freight Transport Planning and Logistics. Proceedings, 1987. X, 568 pages. 1988.

Vol. 318: T. Doup, Simplicial Algorithms on the Simplotope. VIII, 262 pages. 1988.

Vol. 319: D.T. Luc, Theory of Vector Optimization. VIII, 173 pages. 1989.

Vol. 320: D. van der Wijst, Financial Structure in Small Business. VII, 181 pages. 1989.

Vol. 321: M. Di Matteo, R.M. Goodwin, A. Vercelli (Eds.), Technological and Social Factors in Long Term Fluctuations. Proceedings. IX, 442 pages. 1989.

Vol. 322: T. Kollintzas (Ed.), The Rational Expectations Equilibrium Inventory Model. XI, 269 pages. 1989.

Vol. 323: M.B.M. de Koster, Capacity Oriented Analysis and Design of Production Systems. XII, 245 pages. 1989.

Vol. 324: I.M. Bomze, B.M. Pötscher, Game Theoretical Foundations of Evolutionary Stability. VI, 145 pages. 1989.

Vol. 325: P. Ferri, E. Greenberg, The Labor Market and Business Cycle Theories. X, 183 pages. 1989.

Vol. 326: Ch. Sauer, Alternative Theories of Output, Unemployment, and Inflation in Germany: 1960–1985. XIII, 206 pages. 1989.

Vol. 327: M. Tawada, Production Structure and International Trade. V, 132 pages. 1989.

Vol. 328: W. Güth, B. Kalkofen, Unique Solutions for Strategic Games. VII, 200 pages. 1989.

Vol. 329: G. Tillmann, Equity, Incentives, and Taxation. VI, 132 pages. 1989.

Vol. 330: P.M. Kort, Optimal Dynamic Investment Policies of a Value Maximizing Firm. VII, 185 pages. 1989.

Vol. 331: A. Lewandowski, A.P. Wierzbicki (Eds.), Aspiration Based Decision Support Systems. X, 400 pages. 1989.

Vol. 332: T.R. Gulledge, Jr., L.A. Litteral (Eds.), Cost Analysis Applications of Economics and Operations Research. Proceedings. VII, 422 pages. 1989.

Vol. 333: N. Dellaert, Production to Order. VII, 158 pages. 1989.

Vol. 334: H.-W. Lorenz, Nonlinear Dynamical Economics and Chaotic Motion. XI, 248 pages. 1989.

Vol. 335: A.G. Lockett, G. Islei (Eds.), Improving Decision Making in Organisations. Proceedings. IX, 606 pages. 1989.

Vol. 336: T. Puu, Nonlinear Economic Dynamics. VII, 119 pages. 1989.

Vol. 337: A. Lewandowski, I. Stanchev (Eds.), Methodology and Software for Interactive Decision Support. VIII, 309 pages. 1989.

Vol. 338: J.K. Ho, R.P. Sundarraj, DECOMP: an Implementation of Dantzig-Wolfe Decomposition for Linear Programming. VI, 206 pages.

Vol. 339: J. Terceiro Lomba, Estimation of Dynamic Econometric Models with Errors in Variables. VIII, 116 pages. 1990.

Vol. 340: T. Vasko, R. Ayres, L. Fontvieille (Eds.), Life Cycles and Long Waves. XIV, 293 pages. 1990.

Vol. 341: G.R. Uhlich, Descriptive Theories of Bargaining. IX, 165 pages. 1990.

Vol. 342: K. Okuguchi, F. Szidarovszky, The Theory of Oligopoly with Multi-Product Firms. V, 167 pages. 1990.

Vol. 343: C. Chiarella, The Elements of a Nonlinear Theory of Economic Dynamics. IX, 149 pages. 1990.

Vol. 344: K. Neumann, Stochastic Project Networks. XI, 237 pages. 1990.

Vol. 345: A. Cambini, E. Castagnoli, L. Martein, P Mazzoleni, S. Schaible (Eds.), Generalized Convexity and Fractional Programming with Economic Applications. Proceedings, 1988. VII, 361 pages. 1990.

Vol. 346: R. von Randow (Ed.), Integer Programming and Related Areas. A Classified Bibliography 1984–1987. XIII, 514 pages. 1990.

Vol. 347: D. Ríos Insua, Sensitivity Analysis in Multi-objective Decision Making. XI, 193 pages. 1990.

Vol. 348: H. Störmer, Binary Functions and their Applications. VIII, 151 pages. 1990.

Vol. 349: G.A. Pfann, Dynamic Modelling of Stochastic Demand for Manufacturing Employment. VI, 158 pages. 1990.

Vol. 350: W.-B. Zhang, Economic Dynamics. X, 232 pages. 1990.

Vol. 351: A. Lewandowski, V. Volkovich (Eds.), Multiobjective Problems of Mathematical Programming. Proceedings, 1988. VII, 315 pages. 1991.

Vol. 352: O. van Hilten, Optimal Firm Behaviour in the Context of Technological Progress and a Business Cycle. XII, 229 pages. 1991.

Vol. 353: G. Ricci (Ed.), Decision Processes in Economics. Proceedings, 1989. III, 209 pages 1991.

Vol. 354: M. Ivaldi, A Structural Analysis of Expectation Formation. XII, 230 pages. 1991.

Vol. 355: M. Salomon. Deterministic Lotsizing Models for Production Planning. VII, 158 pages. 1991.

Vol. 356: P. Korhonen, A. Lewandowski, J . Wallenius (Eds.), Multiple Criteria Decision Support. Proceedings, 1989. XII, 393 pages. 1991.

Vol. 357: P. Zörnig, Degeneracy Graphs and Simplex Cycling. XV, 194 pages. 1991.

Vol. 358: P. Knottnerus, Linear Models with Correlated Disturbances. VIII, 196 pages. 1991.

Vol. 359: E. de Jong, Exchange Rate Determination and Optimal Economic Policy Under Various Exchange Rate Regimes. VII, 270 pages. 1991.

Vol. 360: P. Stalder, Regime Translations, Spillovers and Buffer Stocks. VI, 193 pages . 1991.

Vol. 361: C. F. Daganzo, Logistics Systems Analysis. X, 321 pages. 1991.

Vol. 362: F. Gehrels, Essays In Macroeconomics of an Open Economy. VII, 183 pages. 1991.

Vol. 363: C. Puppe, Distorted Probabilities and Choice under Risk. VIII, 100 pages . 1991

Vol. 364: B. Horvath, Are Policy Variables Exogenous? XII, 162 pages. 1991.

Vol. 365: G. A. Heuer, U. Leopold-Wildburger. Balanced Silverman Games on General Discrete Sets. V, 140 pages. 1991.

Vol. 366: J. Gruber (Ed.), Econometric Decision Models. Proceedings, 1989. VIII, 636 pages. 1991.

Vol. 367: M. Grauer, D. B. Pressmar (Eds.), Parallel Computing and Mathematical Optimization. Proceedings. V, 208 pages. 1991.

Vol. 368: M. Fedrizzi, J. Kacprzyk, M. Roubens (Eds.), Interactive Fuzzy Optimization. VII, 216 pages. 1991.

Vol. 369: R. Koblo, The Visible Hand. VIII, 131 pages. 1991.

Vol. 370: M. J. Beckmann, M. N. Gopalan, R. Subramanian (Eds.), Stochastic Processes and their Applications. Proceedings, 1990. XLI, 292 pages. 1991.

Vol. 371: A. Schmutzler, Flexibility and Adjustment to Information in Sequential Decision Problems. VIII, 198 pages. 1991.

Vol. 372: J. Esteban, The Social Viability of Money. X, 202 pages. 1991.

Vol. 373: A. Billot, Economic Theory of Fuzzy Equilibria. XIII, 164 pages. 1992.

Vol. 374: G. Pflug, U. Dieter (Eds.), Simulation and Optimization. Proceedings, 1990. X, 162 pages. 1992.

Vol. 375: S.-J. Chen, Ch.-L. Hwang, Fuzzy Multiple Attribute Decision Making. XII, 536 pages. 1992.

Vol. 376: K.-H. Jöckel, G. Rothe, W. Sendler (Eds.), Bootstrapping and Related Techniques. Proceedings, 1990. VIII, 247 pages. 1992.

Vol. 377: A. Villar, Operator Theorems with Applications to Distributive Problems and Equilibrium Models. XVI, 160 pages. 1992.

Vol. 378: W. Krabs, J. Zowe (Eds.), Modern Methods of Optimization. Proceedings, 1990. VIII, 348 pages. 1992.

Vol. 379: K. Marti (Ed.), Stochastic Optimization. Proceedings, 1990. VII, 182 pages. 1992.

Vol. 380: J. Odelstad, Invariance and Structural Dependence. XII, 245 pages. 1992.

Vol. 381: C. Giannini, Topics in Structural VAR Econometrics. XI, 131 pages. 1992.

Vol. 382: W. Oettli, D. Pallaschke (Eds.), Advances in Optimization. Proceedings, 1991. X, 527 pages. 1992.

Vol. 383: J. Vartiainen, Capital Accumulation in a Corporatist Economy. VII, 177 pages. 1992.

Vol. 384: A. Martina, Lectures on the Economic Theory of Taxation. XII, 313 pages. 1992.

Vol. 385: J. Gardeazabal, M. Regúlez, The Monetary Model of Exchange Rates and Cointegration. X, 194 pages. 1992.

Vol. 386: M. Desrochers, J.-M. Rousseau (Eds.), Computer-Aided Transit Scheduling. Proceedings, 1990. XIII, 432 pages. 1992.

Vol. 387: W. Gaertner, M. Klemisch-Ahlert, Social Choice and Bargaining Perspectives on Distributive Justice. VIII, 131 pages. 1992.

Vol. 388: D. Bartmann, M. J. Beckmann, Inventory Control. XV, 252 pages. 1992.

Vol. 389: B. Dutta, D. Mookherjee, T. Parthasarathy, T. Raghavan, D. Ray, S. Tijs (Eds.), Game Theory and Economic Applications. Proceedings, 1990. ??, ?? pages. 1992.

Vol. 390: G. Sorger, Minimum Impatience Theorem for Recursive Economic Models. X, 162 pages. 1992.

Vol. 391: C. Keser, Experimental Duopoly Markets with Demand Inertia. X, 150 pages. 1992.

Vol. 392: K. Frauendorfer, Stochastic Two-Stage Programming. VIII, 228 pages. 1992.

Vol. 393: B. Lucke, Price Stabilization on World Agricultural Markets. XI, 274 pages. 1992.

Vol. 394: Y.-J. Lai, C.-L. Hwang, Fuzzy Mathematical Programming. XIII, 301 pages. 1992.

Vol. 395: G. Haag, U. Mueller, K. G. Troitzsch (Eds.), Economic Evolution and Demographic Change. XVI, 409 pages. 1992.

Vol. 396: R. V. V. Vidal (Ed.), Applied Simulated Annealing. VIII, 358 pages. 1992.

Vol. 397: J. Wessels, A. P. Wierzbicki (Eds.), User-Oriented Methodology and Techniques of Decision Analysis and Support. Proceedings, 1991. XII, 295 pages. 1993.

Vol. 398: J.-P. Urbain, Exogeneity in Error Correction Models. XI, 189 pages. 1993.

Vol. 399: F. Gori, L. Geronazzo, M. Galeotti (Eds.), Nonlinear Dynamics in Economics and Social Sciences. Proceedings, 1991. VIII, 367 pages. 1993.

Vol. 400: H. Tanizaki, Nonlinear Filters. XII, 203 pages. 1993.

Vol. 401: K. Mosler, M. Scarsini, Stochastic Orders and Applications. V, 379 pages. 1993.

Vol. 402: A. van den Elzen, Adjustment Processes for Exchange Economies and Noncooperative Games. VII, 146 pages. 1993.

Vol. 403: G. Brennscheidt, Predictive Behavior. VI, 227 pages. 1993.

Vol. 404: Y.-J. Lai, Ch.-L. Hwang, Fuzzy Multiple Objective Decision Making. XIV, 475 pages. 1994.

Vol. 405: S. Komlósi, T. Rapcsák, S. Schaible (Eds.), Generalized Convexity. Proceedings, 1992. VIII, 404 pages. 1994.

Vol. 406: N. M. Hung, N. V. Quyen, Dynamic Timing Decisions Under Uncertainty. X, 194 pages. 1994.

Vol. 407: M. Ooms, Empirical Vector Autoregressive Modeling. XIII, 380 pages. 1994.

Vol. 408: K. Haase, Lotsizing and Scheduling for Production Planning. VIII, 118 pages. 1994.

Vol. 409: A. Sprecher, Resource-Constrained Project Scheduling. XII, 142 pages. 1994.

Vol. 410: R. Winkelmann, Count Data Models. XI, 213 pages. 1994.

Vol. 411: S. Dauzère-Péres, J.-B. Lasserre, An Integrated Approach in Production Planning and Scheduling. XVI, 137 pages. 1994.